JUST
STAND

One Family's Supernatural
Journey of Faith

By Sue Nutman

ROOTS AND WINGS
MINISTRIES INTERNATIONAL

Cover and layout done by
Covenant Communication Solutions LLC

ISBN: 978-1-7344293-1-2

Just Stand: One Family's Supernatural Journey of Faith
Copyright © 2020 by Roots and Wings Ministries International

Published by Roots and Wings Ministries International
PO Box 316
5740 North Carefree Circle, Suite 120
Colorado Springs CO 80917

Dedication

First and foremost, I want to dedicate this book to my amazing husband Bryan, I wouldn't have wanted to go on this journey with anyone else. It's an honor to be your wife and best friend. To my two incredible children, Aimee McDaniel and Jonathan Nutman, it was your dedication to follow us as parents on this journey and to trust God along the way which strengthened us. To our faithful family in England, you stood by us even when you didn't always understand.

I also dedicate this book to the many friends in the US and around the world who have in some way been part of this journey: our HMI church family, Pastors Dan and Penny Funkhouser, and all the Charis Bible College instructors who shared such great revelation with us. To all who have worked on this book with me, Eileen Quinn, John Bullock, and Greg Troup, I thank you for your hours of dedication. We thank you and pray a blessing over each of you.

And not forgetting to mention the One without whom this never could have happened. You have shown complete faithfulness to us, Father God, on this journey. ☺

Endorsements

As pastors in full-time ministry, there are many times my wife, Penny, and I have had the opportunity to meet and build relationships with some very amazing couples. Bryan and Sue Nutman are one of those couples. They both have experienced a life-changing process as they discovered the reality of who Jesus Christ truly is.

We have known Sue since 2012 and know she has a heart to see the wounded healed. This book, *Just Stand*, tells the story of how she and her husband, Bryan left England and walked away from all they had to begin a new life in the Spirit. It is a very unusual thing for any wife and mother to walk away from the security of her home and family to follow her husband and learn about our amazing God. Sue shares from her heart about God healing their marriage and how they learned to walk together in forgiveness. Her experience with following God and sharing her story will touch your heart and change your life.

Dan and Penny Funkhouser, Pastors
Heartbeat Ministries International

The Enemy's greatest fear is that we'll discover who we really are, what we're really worth, and what our destiny in Christ really looks like. You will be mesmerized as you read this transparent story of an English family's journey through Charis Bible College. Your innermost being will be touched by the very personal journey with God that transformed Sue's heart. As you read the story unveiled in these pages, you will find the same power to overcome for yourself and truly be set free.

Beth Landt
Former Dean of Women
Charis Bible College Colorado

Contents

Foreword

The age-old cry of mankind is "Why am I here?" Implicit in that cry is, "What am I supposed to be doing?" For Christians today that cry is modified only a little: "Why am I here?" and "What does God want me to be doing?" The people who commit to obey that answer are the ones who will hear from God.

Sue Nutman tells the story of two people who determined to follow God. What followed for herself, her husband, Bryan, and her family was not just a happy story of their stepping into the grand adventure that God had worked out for them. Instead, it was a separation from friends, family, and resources. It was a transition into a strange new country and culture. It was a testing over and over of where their trust lay: whether it was in the circumstances of what they saw or in the character of God and what He told them. Their ultimate destination was unclear and the path was not easy.

The thing I most appreciate about this book is its honesty. This is not a typical Christian feel-good story of God working things out for the Nutmans—because the real story is about God working out the Nutmans for Himself. The surface story may be about the stresses of their physical and cultural move from England to America, but the deeper story tells of their spiritual travails in moving from their old ways of doing things and old support systems to a new dependence on God.

They learned how to talk to Him (sometimes while angry and frustrated) and how to hear His voice and direction, finding Him to be more and more reliable as they went.

My wife, Cheryl, and I were classmates with Sue and Bryan in Bible school. We also attended the same church. As we discovered each other on the same path of leaving our own agendas to follow God without reservation, we gradually became close friends. Until our second year, I was only vaguely aware of the fiscal and emotional struggles they were enduring. What became clear, though, was that they were committed to hearing God, knowing His Word and, once being sure of His direction, following Him wherever, no matter how inconvenient. They also had a passion for others to know God on a personal level, to hear His voice, and to see themselves as God had always seen them: loved, empowered, and called.

For the Nutmans, the Christian life is no longer abstract or impractical. They have been transformed through their walk with God. It's a privilege for all of us to have Sue swing the door open, even in hindsight, so we can see the faithfulness of God behind the scenes.

Their ministry, Roots and Wings Ministries International, was birthed in the crucible of these experiences (Prov. 17:3). Their yielding to the fire of God, along with the Holy Spirit's direction, brought the overflowing life that so many Christians say they long for. Because of their own experience, their ministry is to see believers and ministries awakened to their God-ordained purpose and destiny, moving in the supernatural power and love of God as a lifestyle.

Through the story that Sue so personally and poignantly shares, to the life and relationship behind that lifestyle, to the Person Himself, the path is not always clear or simple, but following God always leads to life. You're invited to join them on that journey.

John W. Bullock, Col (ret), USAF, BSC
Author, *Seeing with Fresh Eyes: Sin, Salvation, and the Steadfast Love of God*
December 2019, Colorado Springs, Colorado

THE SIGNIFICANCE
OF THE HERON
from Ephesians 6:10

A heron will stand for an incredible amount of time, focused in on one spot and on one target. We need to do the same with our faith. Having done all we can do, we need to "just stand."

Make a stand for what you believe in and simply do what God inside is showing you. Stand in spite of judgment, disapproval, or fear of man!

*So therefore, **just stand**.*

Prophetically a heron can mean self-determination, or as I prefer to say, God-determination!

JUST STAND

PART 1

The Journey of a British Family in America

To my great surprise, it's not the destination's end that God is interested in. Instead, it's how the journey transforms the human heart

What you hold in your hand, dear reader, is a journey that started in Bath, England, in August 2009. Correction—it probably started way before that, at the foundation of the world (Eph. 1:4-5).

What follows is my journaled account—as a wife, a mother, a daughter, and a soon-to-be Bible school student—of how God transformed and restored my family's lives.

Our story is chronicled through different phases: the journey to America, college life, family restoration, and new seasons. I'm hoping you will laugh, cry, and grow with me on this journey, much as I have over the last ten years.

Where to start?

Well, dear reader, you probably need me to first give you some essential background. For me it all began with this revelation:

Life begins at forty.

Yes, it really did! Why don't we just jump in here together?

Chapter 1

FORTIETH BIRTHDAY PARTY

August 19, 2009

Tonight, as the drinks flowed amongst all the partygoers, I panned the room and saw friends and family enjoying themselves. Then, a question occurred to me in a strange hollow moment: "Is this my life?" I remembered as a young girl I had thought I would grow up to make a difference in the world.

You see, while the party was carrying on, we looked like a perfect family, but we were only a shell of perfection. To all our guests, we seemed to be able to have what we wanted, with no expense spared. *Look at this party*, I challenged myself. My husband, Bryan, had hired out a whole pub in beautiful south Devon—filled with free booze, food, and fun. Friends had come down to join us for a few days because we were known to throw good parties! But this act we had put on in front of others was wearing thin on both of us. Our home life had deteriorated to the point that Bryan and I were almost living separate lives. We were now both accustomed to wearing masks with family, friends, and one another.

Turning to Bryan across the room, I challenged myself to look at him. He was busy discussing business with the proprietor of the pub. He was most likely promising him access to the best specialized food deals in the UK. As was ordinary, he had a glass in one hand, phone in the other, and was looking up the latest prices. You see, dear reader, Bryan was a successful specialist global food importer for major international companies and hotel chains. His identity had become his job and business. Yet really, he was the perfect example of a "prodigal son." We'll cover this later, and you will understand more about this as we go.

Even as I stood at the party, I had to admit to myself that I looked forward to him traveling away from us with work. Over our last ten years of marriage, I had built a life apart from him: I had my job and my children—Aimee and Jonathan. Bryan was so driven with work; he always had to be the best salesman or top earner of the month.

Don't get me wrong; I used to like all the fine dining in London, the expensive holidays, and the work-social scene, but even those posh experiences were becoming ordinary. Standing in that room in that moment, I just felt empty. Then came a sense of horrid dread: NO ONE must know how I'm feeling. I consciously tried to work out in my mind what would be a good age for the children if we were to leave him. Every time I considered it, I became blocked. The reality is there is no good age to split up a family.

We finished our weekend with friends, and then Bryan surprised me by taking me to the most amazing place, Gidleigh Park, for a couple of nights. It is a Michelin 2-star, 5-star hotel. As I said, no expense was ever spared. And, when Bryan wasn't working, I saw a glimmer of my old Bryan. I know he always wanted the best for me. But just like a lot of families caught up in experiences and consumption, we had grown apart over the years. We had let the cares of the world, bad relationships, and the devil drive us apart.

Chapter 2

THE FIRST CRACK IN THE MASK

My normal Friday evenings whenever Bryan was away were often quite routine. Children were gotten into bed first. I would then make my way to the kitchen where I would pour myself a large glass of wine, preferably a bold cabernet sauvignon, and then to the bedroom, where I would usually just put the telly on. But there it was again, the book my mother had given me on my birthday. It came unwrapped with a word of advice, "Sue, I think you should read this book: *The Shack*." After unpacking it from my bag, it had just laid on my bedstand waiting for me.

A bit about my mum. My faithful mum had given her life to Jesus twenty years earlier, shortly before Bryan and I had gotten married. She was followed by my dad about five years later.

On that particular night as I entered my bedroom, it was almost as if the book was calling to me, in my mum's voice, of course. After scanning the channels and seeing that nothing of interest was on, I decided to pick up *The Shack*.

The book intrigued me. It had an American setting. The main character, Mac, was living a comfortable life, but it was interrupted by tragedy: his youngest girl was kidnapped and killed when he had taken his three children away on weekend. His wife, Nan, who usually managed their schedules, had stayed behind.

After the death of his youngest, Mac could not reconcile himself to his life. There was an irreparable tear, a gaping hole, in the fabric of his family. This struck me with force as I read it. I often felt like I, too, was standing on the edge of tragedy. Mac began to get messages from "God," the first one as a letter in his mailbox. Thinking his neighbor was playing a cruel trick on him, the character deciced that by escaping to a cabin in the woods, would help him alleviate something. However, on the way, a winter storm moves in. Suddenly, he finds himself at a cabin and a "family" is waiting to speak to him.

As I was reading this story, it was the first time I had the thought God was wanting to communicate with me. When Bryan returned from his trip, I spoke to him a bit about it, even suggesting he read the book. To my surprise, he was quiet and thoughtful.

At that time, I did not know that Bryan had given his life to Jesus at age twelve. I would learn later that at age fifteen, he had turned down a dark road. In sum, he had turned his back on God the Father. His parents had been badly hurt by their church, plus other situations involving church religion had turned Bryan away from the Lord. So, at this stage of being married to him for eighteen years, this career-driven-business Bryan was the only man I knew.

Take a step back with me: when we first met at ages eighteen and nineteen, respectively, all he told me of his family's faith was that they were Baptist. That seemed like quite enough of a gap between our two families, bearing in mind that all of my family were Catholic. Once, a mutual friend mentioned that Bryan's parents were *born-again-Jesus-followers* but that they didn't *do church* anymore. Not being familiar with that world, the words were just unfamiliar jargon to me.

In truth, that was all I knew before I married Bryan. He never talked of those years. However, with Bryan being Baptist, it didn't go down very well with his family that I was Catholic. In spite of the difference between us, we were married when I was twenty-one and Bryan was twenty-two. How did we solve the Catholic-Baptist divide? Well, we did it in a proper English manner; let's just say we were married on *mutual ground*, in the Church of England.

Now, as a couple of forty and forty-one, was God trying to tell us something? Of course He was!

In hindsight, it was no coincidence that Bryan's eldest sister, Elizabeth, had come to live with us for a while. She had gotten a job near us with Virgin Communications, in the northeast of Bath. She had given her life to Jesus about two years earlier. Whenever she would drop by, I often overheard her talking to Bryan about her relationship with the Lord. There were times when I would walk in on their conversations as Bryan was saying, "No, I'm not interested." But I was intrigued as to what she was telling him.

As a good Catholic, here is what I knew about church: arrive on time, be respectful to the priest, remember to go to confession, and say your "Hail Marys" when they were assigned. I believed that as long as I was a good person, I might get to heaven. In my own eyes, I was good! I was bringing up the children to believe in God and had had them christened as babies, and we went to church on Christmas and Easter as a family (that was my definition of being good). As far as I was concerned, God was that big guy in the sky making good and bad things happen.

My mum used to tell me about her Bible studies and how they were praying for Bryan and me. She used to use phrases like *relationship with Jesus*. But to me, at that time, it all sounded like another commitment that I didn't have time for.

"Mum, once I'm retired, I will join a church. I haven't got time for coffee mornings and praying."

Of course, I would pray when things were bad: "God, why is my life like this?" "God, make things change." But I lacked an understanding of what a personal relationship with Jesus was, so it was impossible for me to draw upon it in crisis. It was all a mystery to me.

Chapter 3

FOLLOWING MY FORTIETH

Back to life beginning at forty. In the weeks that followed my birthday, this question began to burn in my heart: *Is there more to life than this?* Then, one week towards the end of October, my son, Jonathan, came home from his Friday night children's church group with a question.

As you can see, with my mask on, I was skilled at doing the right things, like sending my son to a children's church group. However, behind the mask, I had no understanding of Jesus myself.

After reading *The Shack*, I had a thought I had never had before. It occurred to me that the notion of "Trinity" that I had learned as a Catholic was different than what I had been introduced to in *The Shack*. This new Trinity was based on relationship. It was very strange to hear my own son realize this at the tender age of nine:

"Mum, do you know Jesus is my friend? And if you come with me next week, you can ask a question at church too."

To which I replied, "That's nice, darling," thinking, *I'm too busy to fit that in*.

You see, my Friday nights were very important to me. While Jonathan went to his church club, I went to my Pilates club. Jonathan's request would mean that I would miss that! But when your nine-year-old tells you he will get a sticker if you go, there is a social pressure to be that "good mum." I maintained in my mind I was, so on October 29, 2009, I went with Elizabeth, Bryan's sister, down to North Bradley Baptist Church's "Big Question Evening." To my great surprise that evening, though I started off born a Catholic then had married by way of the Church of England, I found myself thinking, *Why not try the Baptists?*

The evening was a total setup by God Himself, of course. I only realized later that He had been preparing my heart over the previous few months as my God-chats with Mum and Elizabeth had become longer and longer. All I kept thinking was*, If Jesus is real, does He want a relationship **with me***? Then, as I tried to reason through this new development in my family situation, I began thinking, *Maybe, if I have a relationship with Jesus, it won't matter if I divorce Bryan* (Sue logic). Forgive my wrong thinking, but you can see what a mess I really was!

Over those last few weeks, just before I had gone to church at Jonathan's invitation, Bryan had seemed more distant than ever. I didn't know what it was, but I knew there was major stuff going down with his work. He had started his own company with a partner who was an Indian Sikh. However, the upper management of his former company, for whom he had worked the previous ten years, was not happy. In the specialized food industry, there is huge competition for the same customers. Only a limited number of deals are available in such a niche market. Shall we say, it was a very stressful time for Bryan.

Back to my evening at the Baptist church—I was seated in a room with some dear people as Pastor Ben asked who among the visitors had a question. I just listened as a few exchanges were made between those who were brave enough to ask their questions of Pastor Ben. To my amazement, and slight annoyance, no one was asking *my* question. In the end I told myself, *Just get on with it*, and I put up my hand.

"If I ask Jesus into my life tonight, will I be tested?"

Pastor Ben smiled, "Well yes, probably. But the difference is this—Jesus will be with you."

Suddenly, a thought from *The Shack* came back to me: *Mac, the main character, had gone through the most terrible thing, and God had helped him.* Then almost immediately, another thought followed: *Maybe God could help me and my marriage?* But the only way to find out was through asking Jesus to be my Lord and Savior.

In the next few minutes, my sister-in-law, Elizabeth, and a dear lady prayed the sinner's prayer with me. Suddenly, I felt as if I weren't in the room. I felt like I was standing in the middle of a waterfall. And what I can only describe as a river of peace was washing over me. After that experience was over, I can remember people coming up to me and congratulating me, but I felt as if I weren't really in the room. As we drove back home, I can remember thinking, *I don't care if I get divorced or not, because something changed.*

That night I called Bryan, who was away at a hotel near Heathrow airport. Some big business deal was going down. I can remember thinking, *What am I going to tell him?* As soon as he picked up the phone, I said, "I asked Jesus into my life tonight!"

There was a long silence, and then Bryan said, "We will speak tomorrow when I'm back. Tonight, I need to get right with my Father." I thought, *What a strange thing to say. Is he going to call Grandpa?* That was how we referred to his dad since the children came. (Remember, this was all new to me. I had no idea what my new Father was putting into place for me and my family.)

The next morning, I got up and took the children to school. As I walked my dogs, everything appeared different. The grass, the tree—everything looked like it was sparkling. Thinking back on it later, I realized it was like a veil had been lifted. I felt as if I weren't really in my old life anymore. I now know that the contrast I was perceiving was because the Holy Spirit was within me, but at the time, to be honest, it felt as if I were high!

Chapter 4

A VERY DIFFERENT HOMECOMING

Later that day, Bryan returned home. Sad to say, but I used to dread him coming through the door, especially of late, with all the stress of his business. Normally, he would walk in still on the phone. His business deals often continued straight through dinner and into the evening. But as he came in that night, I looked into his eyes, which were normally dark and angry. However, this night, there was a change. His eyes looked brighter, clearer, and even peaceful in an unfamiliar way.

When the children were asleep, and we were alone, Bryan spoke to me in a way he hadn't in many years.

"So, tell me about your experience last night."

As I explained what happened, he listened. I kept telling him how different things looked to me as I walked the dogs and went about my day. Then quite suddenly, another realization began to wash over me. My normal sense of uneasiness and dread around Bryan, which had been building up for years, was gone! A darkness had lifted off of me.

We had been chatting for a while when Bryan started to open up his heart to me. It was probably the first time since our early years of marriage.

Bryan began by telling me he had had an experience with the Lord in his hotel room the same night after I had told him I had asked Jesus into my heart. Basically, he described how a flood of memories from the past, from when he had had first believed, came rushing back. There was an urgency in that moment to say "yes" again to Jesus. The Lord was calling Bryan back to the plan He had for him before he had run away from Him as a boy of fifteen. Bryan described an experience he had with Father God that night in the hotel room. He was face-down on the carpet, unable to move for hours as the power of God washed over him. He said it was a strange encounter because he knew he had not had a drink that night!

"Oh, wow," I said, not really understanding the complexity of his words. I would learn only later that, like the prodigal son in Luke 15, Bryan's pigpen was a hotel room. After our phone call, he *came to himself* and returned to his heavenly Father, who had been waiting for him for twenty-six years.

Chapter 5

Now with the Reset Button Pushed

Over the next few weeks, things changed quite dramatically between us. We were attending the Baptist church together, and Bryan often spent time chatting with Pastor Ben. Six weeks after giving my life to Jesus, I was water baptized at the church, and Bryan formally rededicated his life. Things were good between us all, apart from twelve-year-old Aimee, who was really struggling with the sudden change in our family dynamic.

She cried on the day of my baptism, not really understanding what was going on. She was used to life being a certain way and had built up her own walls. Her walls helped her cope with how she was feeling about family life. Also during this time, she was being bullied at school. She already felt like the world was against her, and now something really weird had happened to everyone in her family.

Jonathan, on the other hand, was happy as we were all going to *his* church. Big stickers for him! He was also happy because Bryan was spending more time at home.

As far as our extended families were concerned, they could all see that something was changing. At my baptism, there seemed to be a mixture of relief, amazement, confusion, and fear as they witnessed an outside force take hold of us and begin to transform us all.

Jesus continued to work through the door we had opened to Him. We carried on going to church, but Aimee would only come sometimes. Other times, she resisted. The Lord would often tell us to leave her at home. On one such occasion, after we arrived home after church, Aimee met us at the front door in tears, visibly shaken. Looking into her distressed face, I blurted out, "Sorry, darling, I won't go to church any more if it upsets you so." To my surprise, she said, "No, no, Mum. I met Jesus in my bedroom this morning." The three of us sat on the couch in the living room, all crying. It felt as if she would now be joining us on this new journey.

Throughout all of this, there is one thing I am so grateful for—that God spoke to me so clearly from the beginning of my new life with Him. I truly needed it, as you will see. Times would come when all our family had to stand on were the words He had given us, sprinkled like breadcrumbs on an unfamiliar trail. Sometimes, it was even just one crumb of a word!

After Aimee's encounter with God, that Sunday morning things began to change quite quickly. The Lord told me to switch both Aimee and Jonathan from their current schools. It was only in hindsight that we realized just how unhappy Aimee had been there. The children would attend the same school a Christian one about six miles away from where we were living. Strangely, I had never heard of it until I went to our new church. It was called Emmaus School, and it had only sixty children in total, ages 5-16. Jonathan joined a class of ten children, while Aimee joined a class of just four! This was in May 2010, six months after I had given my life to Jesus.

Over the next few months, life was pretty good. Bryan and I were getting to know each other again, and we were getting the children settled. Both of our extended families were seeing changes in us, although not always understanding them. Bryan was working to rebuild the relationships with his family that had all but drifted apart.

On the job front, things were heating up for Bryan in his business, though. He didn't want to travel as much or stay away from home. Because of the changes in Bryan, he was no longer comfortable doing business "the old way." Bryan became aware of Proverbs 11:1 NKJV, "Dishonest scales are an abomination to the Lord, but a just weight is His delight." Thereafter, there were business deals that he couldn't follow through with. In addition, he was no longer as much fun because he wouldn't attend the after-hours parties. People began to tell him they didn't know him anymore.

Eventually, the Lord clearly showed us to let the business go. This was very out of character for Bryan; the old Bryan would not have even considered the idea. Instead, he would have fought it all the way. But we both wanted to do what the Lord wanted us to do, even if it cost us.

During the same time period, our Baptist church was going through changes in leadership. As we observed Pastor Ben going through a transition with the elders and deacons, we learned how political church organizations could be. I'm sure this is not Jesus's heart at all. Ben, who knew how Bryan's family had been hurt by the church politics, released us from the church with his blessing. We then joined Elizabeth's church, which was a Vineyard church lead by Pastors Jason and Samantha. This was a younger church, and our children settled well into the children and youth groups.

At this time, I began helping in the children's ministry. Since I had been educated as an early years practitioner, I was a natural fit for that role. Bryan began to serve as operations lead. As our friendships in the church grew, some of our older friends found the "new Sue and Bryan" to be a challenge. We were different.

It's so funny how our lives transformed once we had made that commitment to the Lord. We no longer wanted or needed those extravagant parties. Other things began to change as well. I began to be aware of how little we used to speak to each other and how consumed we were with material comforts. I became aware that with Jesus living in me, it wasn't only that some of our previous actions were now not appropriate; we no longer desired our old lifestyle.

We discovered 2 Corinthians 5:17 NKJV, "Therefore, if anyone is in Christ, he is a new creation; old things have passed away; behold, all things have become new."

Chapter 6

NEW INSTRUCTIONS

By December, Bryan's business was really becoming a strain on him. He was constantly clashing with his business partner, and he began to realize that it was a spiritual battle. Now, with a Christian mindset, he could not negotiate conflict in the same way.

During this time, Aimee and I were visiting my parents in Devon. We were walking the dogs and talking about Bryan's sister, Elizabeth. She had announced that she would be to going to a Bible college in America—Bethel Church's School of Supernatural Ministry in Redding, California. Her choice seemed scary yet liberating at the same time. As Aimee and I were chatting about her dad's situation, we sensed a change for our family was coming as well.

I said to Aimee, "I'm not sure what Dad will do about the business. Maybe we can sell our share and move to Devon."

Aimee said, "Why Devon, Mum?"

"Yes," I persisted, "we can sell the house, move to Devon, and buy a tea shop and sell Christian books and music. Don't you see, Aimz? I love Devon. My parents are here. I love the coastline and the pretty villages...God wants us in Devon! "

Aimee in her thirteen-year-old wisdom said, "That's sounds like you, Mum, not God!"

"Maybe He hasn't said that, but He has told me that your dad is going to be in ministry... So, why not Devon!"

Then Aimee insisted, "God told me we will be living in America!"

"America," I said. "Don't be silly. Why would God take us to America?? Aunty Elizabeth is going there. That's her journey, not ours!"

We had a good Christmas that year. Things were different. There was more meaning to the season than there had ever been before. But I sensed Bryan was still very uneasy with the business situation. I prayed, "Lord, show us what to do. Give Bryan a new direction." (All the while, I was secretly praying that it would be a relocation to Devon!)

March 7, 2011

By the end of February, Bryan was having to make a decision about the business. Communication between him and his business partner had become critical.

On the March 7, 2011, as Bryan was getting out of bed, the Lord said, "You're done."

Bryan asked, "Done with what?"

He told Bryan that this would be the day he was to come out of the business.

Bryan phoned his company's financial director to say he was leaving the business. Within twenty-four hours, he was cut off from everything.

At the time, I buried my head a bit. I remember thinking, *He's not really just going to walk away from all that he has built, is he?* But I had to trust Bryan, and God. He said he was following what the Lord was showing him. So, my first real test on provision was coming up.

On that same day, we were waiting on permits to extend our home's property. We had been waiting two years for these plans to come through. We lived on a sixteenth-century farm estate on 196 acres of land, in a home that had been restored from an old stable block. The estate was home to six other residences, all of which preserved the historical structures of the original farm. It was situated just nine miles outside of Bath, in the county of Wiltshire, and was a beautiful place to live and to raise children.

We needed a permit to extend into the roof to create more living space. But the planning was going backwards and forwards due to historic restoration requirements. The same day he left the business, Bryan received a call from our architect saying, "Good news, Bryan, the permit is finally through." At that exact moment, Bryan heard an audible voice say,

"The house is to be sold."

As you can imagine, Bryan's thoughts were *Sue is going to go mad... I've just walked away from the business and now the Lord wants us to sell the house— her pride and joy! Wow, Lord, what is happening?*

Chapter 7

DROPPING THE BOMB

Over the next couple of weeks, we had a lot of questions for the Lord. Bryan was quiet.

He tells me now his head was spinning with all that was going on. I prayed, but the Lord was quiet, apart from giving me scriptures like Proverbs 3:5-6 and Jeremiah 29:11-12.

Being a new believer and hearing so clearly in those first few months, I was under the false assumption that my relationship with the Lord would always work the same way. When answers didn't seem to flow instantly to me, I began to struggle with what our future would look like. We had enough savings to carry us for probably a year. Whenever fearful thoughts arose, I would tell myself, *Bryan must simply get a different job.* Knowing that he was also feeling the pressure, I thought I would leave it a few weeks before I mentioned my Devon plan! In the meantime, I had my job, as a special needs coordinator in a preschool, which I loved. *Well, I could do that anywhere, couldn't*

I? Then I'd bounce the other way: *There I go again—Sue planning everything!*

You see this desire of mine started when I was young. I ran a family business for fifteen years with my parents. One thing I knew how to do was to make plans and handle people! All through my life I was drawn to jobs that required planning and organizing. Even working in an early-year teaching environment required a lot of planning. I had to be as organized when dealing with two- to five-year-old children as I did when I ran the bakery with Mum and Dad.

I began to see how even before I believed in Him, God was directing our steps. So, it was only over time that I realized that the Lord was moving us along His plan in different ways. For example, Bryan began to repair his relationship with his parents. God began to open up the communication channels that, from years of Bryan doing his own thing, had closed. Over many years, he had grown distant towards them because of his own choices. Only looking back now did I realize that it had been the devil's hand in all of it.

At family get-togethers, there was always tension, usually because Bryan hadn't called or updated his family on when he would arrive or when he planned to leave. For example, on his fortieth birthday, Bryan agreed to take everyone to a hotel in Bristol. During the meal out, Bryan was not engaging with everyone. Suddenly, he stands up and announced that he was heading to a casino. So, for a few of us, there was no choice but to head back to the hotel; a casino was no place for children. But again, Bryan only considered himself, and it always resulted in a tangible tension in the atmosphere for everyone. As Bryan reflects back now on the way he was living, he says his focus was on his job and lifestyle, not his family and all the hassle he created that went with that.

However, after Bryan's encounter with his heavenly Father in the hotel room late in October 2009, I could see his heart begin to soften toward his family relationships. It was like butter being left out of the fridge and softening. Since the time his heart changed, Bryan was actually listening to his family when they spoke. Most surprising was how his attitude changed toward his mother.

Because he was now more open to his mother's suggestions, when Bryan's parents said they were planning on attending the Charis Bible College UK Campus Days in Walsall, Bryan at least considered her words. She said she felt the Lord tell her to invite Bryan (we later found out Bryan's mother operates quite heavily in the prophetic). She said it would be a good place for him to go and seek the Lord for his next step. However, I was still praying the Lord would tell him to move the family to Devon!

So, on March 23, 2011, only two weeks after he had given up the business and the Lord had told him to sell our home, he was sitting in Charis Bible College UK in Walsall. I remember thinking back to the early days of my salvation when the Lord told me Bryan was going into ministry. *Well, I hope that doesn't mean we have to move to the Midlands. I wanted to head south, not north!*

As the meeting started, Wendell Parr was teaching. The first scripture he taught from was Proverbs 11:1, "God dislikes dishonest scales." The irony of that was not lost on Bryan: The Lord had given Bryan that scripture a few months earlier when He asked Bryan to come out of the business. Then, Wendell went on to teach out of the book of Galatians. When the morning session finished, Bryan felt the Lord stirring in his heart. As he was leaving the session, a woman came up to him and said, "The Lord told me to give you this CD." It was Barry Bennett teaching on Galatians. Within himself, Bryan was realizing, *Okay, Lord. You want me to read Galatians?*

Back in his hotel room, Bryan started to read. He got as far as the fifteenth verse of the first chapter when these words leapt off the page:

> But when it pleased God, who separated me from my mother's womb, and called me by his grace, To reveal his Son in me, that I might preach him among the heathen; immediately I conferred not with flesh and blood: Neither went I up to Jerusalem to them which were apostles before me; but I went into Arabia, and returned again unto Damascus. Then after three years I went up to Jerusalem to see Peter, and abode with him fifteen days.
>
> Galatians 1:15-18 (KJV)

As Bryan went back for the evening sessions, he was trying to focus on what the Lord was showing him. *To be separated, what does that mean? And for three years? Lord, do you want me to come to Charis Bible College in Walsall?*

In a vague way, Bryan knew that Charis Bible College (Charis) was related to Andrew Wommack Ministries (AWM), a ministry his parents had been supporting for years. During worship, the two big screens were showing a picture of the world and the AWM logo.

Bryan thought, *So, Lord you want me to study here?*

To his surprise, he audibly heard the Lord say, "Go to the source."

"You are the source, Lord," Bryan responded.

"Go to the source of the ministry."

Bryan responded, "That's America!"

The Lord simply responded to Bryan, "Yes"

As you can imagine, Bryan felt sick. He thought, *Sue is going to be mad. How will we manage this, too, with all the stress of the business situation?* But as you know, if you've ever experienced a clear knowing and sense of direction from God, once He speaks to you in your spirit, He doesn't let it rest.

Another question he had was, *What's Sue going to say? I just walked away from the business. She doesn't know yet that we have to sell the house, and* **now** *You want me to tell her we are moving to America? No, Lord! This is crazy.* With all these thoughts going through his head, he told his parents he wasn't going to stay in Walsall that night. So, Bryan left to drive back home.

Bryan didn't arrive back home until after midnight. The next morning, I was surprised to see him up as I was taking the children to school on my way to work. He didn't seem that talkative.

People, especially family members, were beginning to ask what Bryan was going to do now that he had given up the business. I put a brave face on, saying, "Well, we are trusting and believing we will be shown what comes next."

Have you ever been in our shoes? On the one hand, you have no idea what to do next; on the other hand, the Lord has sown a crazy seed in your heart that you can't tell anyone!

As you can imagine, Bryan realized he'd better have a serious conversation with the Lord: *That was a crazy twenty-four hours. I'll need more to tell Sue than just that we are going to America. You know what she's like; she will want a plan!*

No sooner had he had this internal conversation with Father God, Bryan picked up *Word for Today*, a monthly magazine that we had at home. He opened it up hoping to find some divine inspiration, and there, he came face to face with an advert for Andrew Wommack's television program being aired at 2 a.m. (Bryan later said he was sure he had never seen it advertised in there before or since!) So, Bryan thought, *Well, I suppose it's worth setting up the recording and see what this Andrew Wommack is like. I need something more, Lord, than the last twenty-four hours as a sign.*

After the kids and I were gone for the day, Bryan made a cup of tea and thought, *Right, Mr. Wommack. Let's see what you have to say for yourself.*

As the program started and Andrew announced that he wasn't going to teach today, Bryan thought, *You've got to be kidding me! He's not going to teach!* Instead, Andrew went on to say he wanted to spend the next twenty minutes talking about Charis Colorado and how he had just brought a property in Woodland Park. It was going to be the site of Charis Bible College. The Lord said, *"Do you want any more signs, Bryan?"*

As Bryan related all this to me, you can imagine I wasn't receiving it very well. On the inside, I was thinking, *What? We're moving to America? I'm Okay with you going into ministry or studying, but we are not moving (well, only to Devon). Elizabeth is the one going to America, not us!*

I could suddenly see my world falling into free fall: what about our house, the children, the dogs? Actually, we were walking the dogs when Bryan broke the news to me. At the time, my children will tell you, the dogs were the first concern I mentioned. I was lobbing questions at Bryan faster than a tennis-ball machine at a novice tennis player. He was trying to catch each of my concerns but finally said, "I don't know, Sue. I can't give you those answers. You will have to pray and seek the Lord yourself."

"Too true," I said. "We will see what God is going to say about this!"

Personally, I thought Bryan was going quite insane.

Sure enough, once I calmed down and had some quiet time, I was reading in Ephesians, and the Lord spoke to me through Ephesians 1:4-15. Through that passage, the Lord basically showed me that we were predestined for a plan He had for us. Just like He had shown Bryan through Galatians, He communicated to me that we had to go away for a time to be trained and equipped. I didn't understand why this had to be our plan, and my emotions were all over the place. For one thing, I didn't think I could move away from my family. They had become my rock over the years, and now the Lord wanted me to trust Him. Suddenly in this process, it occurred to me, *I don't even know where Colorado is in America!*

Throughout this process, I had so many questions about why and how? All Bryan kept saying was we needed to trust Him. He admitted that he didn't understand how this would work, either, but he would say he was confident that God would show us. How many of you know that strategy doesn't work for a planner? I wanted answers!

Chapter 8

IN THE AFTERMATH

We sat on the decision for another couple of weeks. During this time, I discovered a strange peace was resting on my heart. I knew emotionally this was going to be the hardest thing I had done so far in my life. But every time I was tempted to fear, I encountered this peace.

We told Aimee and Jonathan our plans to sell the house and go to America. Aimee had a small *I-told-you-so* moment as she reminded me of the word she had been given. Looking back, both children were incredible. They had already witnessed huge changes in both Bryan and me over the previous eighteen months, and life had also changed for them on their own journeys with the Lord. We suggested that no one say anything to family at this stage until we had some more answers.

It was now April 2011. In May, we knew we were going to take the children to the Grace and Faith

Conference put on by Andrew Wommack Ministries at the Charis Bible College in Telford, England. We would all hear Andrew speak there. Unbelievably, we hadn't yet heard him teach!

In the weeks that followed, Bryan was beginning to communicate with Charis Colorado on the admissions process for internationals. There seemed to be a lot to do in a short space of time. The biggest question looming was, could we make September enrollment or would we have to wait for November? A lot would depend on our house sale. (Yes, dear reader, I finally agreed.) Selling a house is a very different process in England as compared with America, as you will find out. I said to Bryan, I'm not leaving until the house is sold and our money is in the bank. That way I could plan out the next three years, as Bryan said we were only going for three years. My plan was still to come back and open a tea room in Devon. Better still, by then Bryan could minister in it!

The next few weeks were really hard as we started to tell family of our plans to go to America. Looking back, we probably didn't handle this time very well. It was very emotional, and it was challenging that we didn't have the answers to the questions they were asking. Just saying that God had told us to go was hard for them to get their heads around. Let's just say there were lots of tears, and not just from me! But again, despite all the heartache, I felt we were doing the right thing.

Chapter 9

God Confirms

Looking back, we had some crazy God-times during those months; He was constantly showing us stuff to keep us on track to go to the United States. We still hadn't said anything to our church family or friends of our plans.

Something interesting happened when a Bethel Church–lead mission team came to a church near us to minister. Our friend Fiona and a couple called Jenny and Andrew told us about it. We suggested that Bryan's sister, Elizabeth, come along, as she would be heading for Redding that September. As we walked into the room, two guys from Bethel were on the stage, ministering. I was sitting with Elizabeth when the Lord said to me, *"Elizabeth's husband is in the room."*

Wow, I thought, *that's a strange thing to hear. I wonder who it would be.* I looked at the two guys on the stage and wondered if it could be the blond guy. He looked like her type; he was quite buff. Then I didn't think anything more of it. The evening went a crazy way with a fire tunnel and people falling out in the spirit, which I thought was weird. Bryan and my friend Fiona seemed to have been affected, but I was not. I have learned since then that the presence of the Holy Spirit can affect people in very different ways, and it's not our place to judge.

I would find out only later that Bryan had a God-experience that night. He perceived God was downloading a supernatural strength into him to deal with the next few months. It's funny that although I was with him, I had no idea he was going through this. I slept peacefully that night while Bryan had a six-hour encounter with the Holy Spirit, so much so, that his body was being completely taken over by the Holy Spirit, massive surges of electricity and power. During this time, he was laughing and shaking with the effects of the Holy Spirit on his body. In the morning he said, "Did you hear or feel anything last night?"

"No," I said. "I slept like a baby!"

"Wow" was his only reply!

Inwardly, I wished I had received the supernatural level of faith that I was going to need over the next few months.

A couple of days later, Jenny and Andrew from our church asked us over to dinner. As we drove over, we decided we weren't going to say anything about America, since still no one from the church knew our plans. I also told Bryan what I felt the Lord had shown me about Elizabeth's husband being in the room. Bryan smiled and asked, "Did he tell you which one?"

"I bet it's that blond buff guy," I said.

"Nope, it's Daniel, the other guy with dark hair."

Bryan explained that as Elizabeth and Daniel were chatting to each other about Elizabeth going to Bethel in September, the Lord said to Bryan, *He's the one.*

We both marveled at how God was speaking so clearly and intimately to us both.

"I don't think we should say anything," I said. "Let's just see if we heard right."

I won't keep you in suspense. Not long after that evening, Elizabeth wanted to have a chat with us. She said that she and Daniel had been chatting on FaceTime over the last month.

"Really?" we said.

"Yes," Elizabeth said, "and he may come back next month for a visit."

Daniel did, and he met the rest of the family. Elizabeth and Daniel were engaged that summer before she left for Bethel! They then went on to be married at Bethel in May of 2012. Daniel had always had a heart for England. After Elizabeth completed two years at Bethel, they returned to England happily married and currently have four beautiful children. God is good!

Anyway, back to our evening. We sat down to dinner and Jenny said to us, "So, what are your plans?"

Bryan and I looked at each other. We weren't ready to say anything to the church yet. We wanted to get the Grace and Faith Conference under our belts first. I wanted to make sure I liked this guy, Andrew Wommack.

Jenny followed her inquiry by saying, "I know where you are going!"

I looked at Bryan as if to say, *Have you said something to them?* His eyes held the same question for me. Finally, Bryan replied to Jenny, "Oh, you do? Where?"

"You will all be in America by the end of the year. God showed me that while you were sitting in front of us last weekend at the Bethel conference."

This was just one more confirmation from God that was spoken to us through others. Since the Lord had already shown them our secret, we filled them in on what we knew of the journey so far. Then after a short discussion, we all prayed. They felt God would continue to confirm His plan for us through other people if we were obedient to listen.

The following weekend was the AWM Grace and Faith Conference in Telford. We had decided to split the weekend as our church was having an activity that same weekend. So, we drove up to Telford on Friday to hear Andrew Wommack and Wendell Parr teach on Saturday.

As Andrew spoke, I can remember thinking, *This man sounds so American. I don't think I can understand him!* But we even managed to speak to him at the end and explain we were planning on coming to Colorado. He told us, "Well, you can do it here if you want."

I can remember thinking, *Should we?*

Then he said, "Well, if you make it, we would be happy to see you."

He spoke in what we would come to love as such a casual Andrew-way!

I spoke also with Wendell. I liked Wendell because he loved England. I bought the book *Sharper Than a Two-Edged Sword* as I felt I needed to read at least one of Andrew's books.

The first thing in the morning, we got up to drive to our church's activity weekend. As we were on our way, I tried to understand what I was feeling. I wouldn't say I had a total peace after the conference. In fact, I think I had more questions than answers. As we were driving, I kept thinking, *Father, do you really want us to go to America?* As I listened to see if I heard an immediate response, I remembered the one thing that really caught my heart that weekend. It was a testimony from a mother whose children were both diagnosed with autism. She had been following Andrew's teaching, believing the Word, and putting into practice what she was hearing. It's a great healing journey, as both of her boys were healed from autism. One of them, Tim, went on to spend three years at Charis Colorado, going through the program.

The reality of this really hit home with me as I had been trained to work with autistic children. I knew how hard it was to first get them diagnosed, and then this woman had seen her children healed and taken off the statement register. There must be something in what Andrew was teaching. I wanted to learn more about this "believer's authority" he was talking about.

When we arrived at our church weekend, we realized we were the last to arrive. I was still asking for more signs and confirmation. Our church friends were wanting to know our plans, especially as we had just come from this conference. "What are the Nutmans going to do?" was the common question from the lips of all who were watching our journey.

As we were approaching the front desk to check-in, I was thinking to myself, *Lord, show me. Is America really where we are supposed to be?* The lady who was checking us into the camp said, "I have one room left. Here's the key. Just go up the stairs to the third door on the right."

As we walked past the first two doors, I notice one door said *Paris,* the other said *Africa*. As we got to our door, it said *Texas*. The four of us just looked at each other as we opened the door to the American-themed room waiting for us. (Nobody at that time knew we were planning on moving to America.)

Chapter 10

PUTTING OUR HOUSE IN ORDER

We took a trip to Wales to visit my great aunt Audie. She's always had a special place in my heart. I lost both my grandmothers at the age of 18, so she filled the gap in my heart.

Aunt Audie had always been an adventurer. When the rest of my family were struggling with our decision to move to America, she thought it was going to be quite exciting. When we saw her, she had been feeling poorly but wouldn't really tell anyone what was wrong.

I have always loved my trips to Wales. She lived on the west Pembrokeshire coast, which is stunningly beautiful. Its beauty is accented by long, curved expanses of beaches with great white cresting waves, quite perfect for surfing. The beaches there have a wild feel to them. With steep black cliffs, they are dotted with great pubs to stop and have fish and chips. As we all sat on the beach, eating our fish and chips, I had a feeling I wouldn't be seeing her again. I promised to keep her posted on our journey. It was emotional as we said our goodbyes.

The next few months were a bit of a blur; the house was on the market. Our families were still trying to come to terms with what we were doing. Bryan was gathering the necessary paperwork for the visa process. I was trying to keep everything together emotionally with everyone. (Why is it that people always go to the women for answers?!)

With the house on the market, we had a guy come and view the house. He fell in love with it straightaway. This had to be God. He too was from America and was wanting a place to live in England. He had a sister living only seven miles away from us. How perfectly God found us a buyer! The American was even willing to work to our timescale. I thought, *Perfect, God, You are so good*. **But actually, we never asked God if this was good.** We just assumed it. Remember that as we venture on into the story! We will call him Mr. P.A.

So, in August of 2011, we headed off to London for our first visa interview. Elizabeth had hers in June. She had no problems and passed straight through. She was off to Bethel on September 6.

As the four us sat in the American embassy, I had a feeling of uneasiness. I kept thinking, *God, you have this*, but I had this inner fear that just would not go away.

Up we went to the first window, number six—*Great*, I thought, *I don't like the number six!* They went through our stuff and told us to sit back down. We were told we would be called by a consulate for the interview. After another forty-five minutes, our number was called window 18. *Great*, I thought, *it's a multiple of six - 666!* The official looked at our paperwork and asked, "Why are you going to America?"

"Well, you see, we feel called by God to study there."

"Really," was her stern reply. "And where will you live? Where will your children go to school? How will you support yourselves?"

As international students in America, we would not be allowed to be employed. We would have to self-fund ourselves. So, this interview was not going well. Bryan tried to explain how we were selling our house, and we would go out and find schools and a house to live in. It was all to no avail; she announced, "I'm going to deny your application. You may leave the embassy now!"

Have you ever had that feeling, as if your world has just come crashing down? Yep, that was us.

We stood there in a stupor as the implication of what just happened washed over us. We had just spent the last few months building the children up, telling them that they were moving to America only to be told "no" at the embassy. As we left the embassy, Jonathan was crying and saying, "You said we were going to America!" Aimee, looking shocked, said, "God told me we would be going to America." I couldn't even process in that moment, so I let Bryan talk with them. My mind was spinning. *Had all the last few months been a delusion? Was all this just a dream? Was it even worth it, now? What in the world comes next, Lord?*

I suddenly felt as if I was not in London. I looked out at the park in front of the embassy. I suddenly remembered that Elizabeth had come with us for support. As Bryan was relaying everything to her, she was hugging Aimee and Jonathan. I became aware that I wasn't really there. I was standing on a glass floor, looking out over the Grand Canyon in America. I can remember thinking, *Is this in Colorado?* I was aware that it was the four of us now standing on this glass floor holding hands, saying, "We've made it." I could even feel the warm dry air on my face! I would only understand later that I was having an open vision.

As you can imagine, once word got out regarding our rejection, friends and family were wanting to know what we were going to do next. I told Bryan about my vision. I didn't understand it, but I thought, *Do you think God wants us to give up? No!* We took stock of where we were. We still had Mr. P.A. wanting our house even though he had gone back to America. He said he would start the process in September, when he returned.

Bryan said, "I feel it would be good for you and I to go to Colorado and see the college. Let's look at schools and for a house to live in. That way if we have those questions asked again, we can answer them."

Of course, the people at the embassy were saying it's harder to get a visa if you have already been refused one. But our God was bigger than that. Plus, He hadn't shown us a plan B. Despite some reservations, we booked a week's trip to Colorado for the first week of September, after Bryan's youngest sister, Rebekah, had gotten married. At about this same time, Elizabeth headed off to Bethel. As you can imagine, this was a very emotional time for both families! This was especially true for Bryan's mother, who had just said goodbye to Elizabeth and was potentially going to be saying goodbye to Bryan too.

Chapter 11

STEPPING OUT OF THE BOAT

Aimee and Jonathan went to stay with my parents as we headed out to Colorado. Bryan and I arrived and booked into a hotel. Our first stop was Charis Bible College, which was then located on Elkton Road, off of Garden of the Gods Road in Colorado Springs. We arrived during orientation week for the first-year students. Students could begin at the end of August, or they could come for a late start in November. We would learn that this second batch of students were called *November students*.

I can remember thinking, *Will I really be here in a few months?* I couldn't stop crying through praise and worship, which was the first hour of school every Monday and Wednesday. People asked if we were going to be students. We said, "Hopefully."

The Americans all responded, That's awesome, just awesome! You will love it."

I kept thinking, *I can't understand what they are saying!*

We then met with the international admissions coordinator. We managed to get an acceptance letter from Charis to help with our visa interview. She prayed with us about the process. We didn't have a date yet for our next interview, as we wanted to get other things in place first. We also decided to come back and sit in on a couple of lessons later that week. That was the first time I heard Barry Bennett teach—very thought provoking. We also heard Andrew Wommack teach on relationship with God. I think that was the first time that I thought, *I can actually see myself here.*

We met up with a real estate lady who was going to show us some rental properties. It was a little hard to find housing, as we were bringing our two dogs with us. Remember, I told Bryan I would not go unless we brought them.

After two or three days and a lot of property viewings, we settled on a house with a private landlord. When we met with the lady, she informed us that her husband was away in Afghanistan, so she was arranging everything alone. We informed her that we had never been renters before either. It took some time to get all the paperwork in place. A lot of trust was required on both sides, as we didn't have an American bank account and no credit rating here. Basically, she trusted us on our word as Christians. She and her husband were amazed when we shared our story to date. It probably helped that since we weren't going to be there until November, we agreed to secure the house with three months' rent up front and sign a year-long contract. Only God knew how we were going to fund two houses! As we parted, we agreed to keep in touch and we took some pictures for Aimee and Jonathan of their new home.

Next, we had to find a school for them. The Lord had very clearly told me that Bryan and I weren't the only ones on a journey. Aimee and Jonathan were on their own journeys. That's why He had told me to move them to the Christian school in our town. After a little searching, Bryan felt that Colorado Springs Christian School was the school to see. We made an appointment with the head teacher. As we explained our situation, I was beginning to get used to the reaction on people's faces when we told them we were doing this on a word from God. Again, being a Christian school, they were excited for us. They had quite a few international students, but none of whom were English. They requested that we arrange a Skype interview with Aimee and Jonathan once we got back. We would need to send all their school records so that they could see what year to put them in. It was an ideal situation at CSCS; Aimee and Jonathan would be together on the same campus, just as they had been in England.

After a busy week of arranging our new life in America, we headed back. I said to Bryan, "Are we crazy? We have just arranged all this stuff, signed away a few thousand dollars on a house and school, but don't even know if we will get through the visa interview again!"

"Well," he said, "God doesn't promise we won't have trials, but He does promise to be with us."

Dear reader, He clearly told me we were being sent to Colorado. I trusted Him. I encouraged myself by looking at how He had spoken to us so far.

Upon returning to the UK, I handed in my notice to my job. It was very hard; I loved the people and the children I worked with. I would leave October 23, just before the half-term break, the same for Aimee and Jonathan. We knew the date we had to be in America was November 28, which was the first day for winter term students. We hoped to get out there a couple of weeks before to set up home and settle the children into CSCS. There was so much to do: pack the house, sort out passports for the dogs, vet visits, plus vaccinations for Aimee and Jonathan. The list went on and on. We couldn't forget that we still had to arrange another visa interview and book flights. This was alongside all the emotions of leaving our family and country.

Family members were wanting to spend any spare time with us, which we didn't seem to have. I developed a driven heart over those weeks. I *had* to get organized. I couldn't stop to think about the emotional side of it, or I would break down.

Mr. P.A. had come back and decided he would take most of our furniture. Apparently, he was divorcing his wife in America, and she was keeping the house and all contents. He even offered us the asking price. This amount would easily give us enough to do the three years of school with some left to invest when we got back. Thank You, Jesus—it was all planned out.

One of the things I had to organize was all of Jonathan's medication. He had been very ill as a baby with severe eczema. It was so severe that I used to have to wrap his little body up every night to help protect him from scratching himself. Then each morning, I would soak off his blood-stained bandages. This lasted until he was about fifteen to eighteen months old. It was a tough time. Basically, I didn't sleep for a year when he was first born.

He had other issues as well, resulting in a few trips to the hospital. A sick child puts a lot of strain on a marriage. By the time he was two, the eczema had eased off, but he began developing asthma. By age eleven, Jonathan was on a regiment of daily medications: an inhaler in the morning and before bed, a steroid tablet daily, a nose spray in the mornings, and an inhaler always on hand during the day. As a result, he was used to self-medicating.

One day, I was standing in the pharmacy waiting to pick up a nine-month supply of asthma medication when I heard a voice say, "He {Jonathan} won't need that in America."

I looked around.

"Was that You, God? Well, I've heard how much medicine costs in America, so I'm taking my own."

As the end of October approached, Bryan said, "Sue, we need to pray for the right date for the interview. We didn't pray last time but just went up there on the first free appointment they had."

I knew Bryan was right. We prayed, but I was getting nothing, not even peace about going! Fear crept in as I was plagued with the thought, *Are we doing the right thing?*

So, we prayed, both together and alone. At the same time, I was also keeping an eye on flights. The closer it was getting towards Thanksgiving, the more the flights to America were going up. We had already signed off a few thousand dollars in Colorado, and our savings balance was going down. Bryan had not worked for six months. Mr. P.A. was looking at exchanging contracts. (This is something you do in England before you close on a property.) He was waiting on funds from America. We were all waiting on America, it seemed!

One morning, as October drew to a close, Bryan said, "Sue, I've been online, and Tuesday, November 3, there is an appointment at the embassy. I have peace about this, so I'm booking it."

I took a deep breath and thought, *Here we go again*. As soon as you book, you must pay $600, and then it's all the other stuff and paperwork. We knew this time would be harder, as we already had a refusal.

I can remember going to bed that night thinking, *Wow, October 29, 2011. Two years ago I gave my life to Jesus. What was it that I asked Pastor Ben? Will I be tested?* I can't believe I was worried if the Lord would ask me to be a missionary in Africa. Things were hard enough trying to go to America!

That night the Lord woke me with the words, **Book the flights.** *What?* I thought. *Am I crazy? No, Lord, not till after our interview*.

The next morning as I was packing up the house, again I heard, **Book the flights.** Again, I responded, *NO!* Then I spoke out loud to Him.

"Lord, do You know how much we are talking about here? It will cost 4,000 pounds for us as a family plus

2,500 pounds for the dogs! If we get refused again, that's another 6,500 pounds we have just thrown away. Plus, my husband isn't working because You want us to go to America to study the Bible together!"

Sometimes you just have to tell God what's going on in your world.

Then I heard, "Do you trust Me? **Book the flights.**"

Sometimes, over the previous few months, I had thoughts that Bryan was crazy when he would tell me things the Lord had communicated to him. I was certain that when I would tell him this, he would think I was crazy. After I got enough nerve, I said, "Bryan, I have something to tell you. God has told me three times now, 'Book the flights.'"

There was an uncomfortable silence as he looked at me. Then he responded, "You've heard from God on this?"

Suddenly, I experienced a righteous anger growing and heard myself say, "Look, I've followed your lead over these last few months. Yes, it's God. He told me to book the flights. I think we should do it. I trust Him!"

Wow, where did that come from? I thought. It even surprised me.

"Okay, let's see what's available," Bryan conceded.

As we searched for available flights, we knew that we had to get a British Airways flight that would be direct to Denver, because of the dogs. Bryan found a flight for all six of us on November 14, leaving from Heathrow, going direct to Denver.

Just before he submitted the payment, he turned to me and asked, "Are you sure, Sue? This is over 6,500 pounds. We don't know the outcome of the interview yet."

I looked at him and said, "God told me!" And, then I thought, *Now, don't You let me down, God!*

"Okay," Bryan responded.

He booked the tickets and then said, "Maybe, we shouldn't say anything to the family about the flights just yet."

I agreed and said, "Let's get through the interview first."

I knew there was no sense making them get out of the boat with us.

The Visa Interview: Take Two

We arrived back in the American embassy, but this time my faith arrived with me, and we were doing it on God's timing.

When our name was called, we were directed to desk number seven. *Well, that's a better start*, I thought to myself. Next, we were called to consulate window twenty-three. We stood before her as she ruffled through all our documents. Finally, after the officer had looked through everything, she asked us, "So, do you have things in place in the US?"

This time we were able to say everything we had put in place on our earlier trip to Colorado. Next the officer asked, "But what will bring you back to the UK after school?"

That was a question we weren't expecting. I searched through what I had rehearsed, and I ventured out a response.

"We will come back to open a Christian ministry. We are just going to Colorado for our training."

"Okay," she said, "I will approve this application."

Thank You, Jesus. Oh, wow, we are going to America in eleven days! I just looked at Bryan and he at me. Oh, my days, this is real!

Our lawyers confirmed that all the paperwork was in place. The house was packed. Mr. P.A. promised he would have all the money in place by November 10. The lawyers said they were just waiting to exchange the contracts before they closed on them, which would occur about two weeks after we arrived in America. This was not my plan; I had wanted everything to be finished before we left, but Mr. P.A. assured us that everything was in good order on his end.

Chapter 12

THE HARD
GOODBYE

November 14, 2011

The next ten days were full of tearful goodbyes with our families. *I feel so guilty for leaving.* This thought would surface at the most inconvenient and emotional moments as we prepared to leave. *Jesus, give me strength to do this*. One small point of consolation was that we had return flights for July 2012. *Sue, you can do this; it's only for nine months.*

I will never forget the drive to Heathrow on the day of our departure. Bryan had all our luggage, and he had headed off to the airport with his parents, his sister Rebekah, and her husband, Tom. They had left from their house, where he had spent the last night with them. I headed out from Devon, as I was at my parents' with Aimee, Jonathan, and the dogs.

I HATE DEPARTURES!

We had to sort the dogs out first; they were going as cargo. So, we loaded them into the crates. They were looking at us as if to say, *What? You lot are crazy!*

My dad and I had an emotional drive to the airport while the children were quiet in the car. There is always a cost to taking a journey with God. That's something you have to think about. You can stand on scriptures like "God will repay in this lifetime, (Mark 10:29) family, land, houses, and relationships," but sometimes things will feel different. I did feel a burden from the decisions we had made to move to America. I just had to trust that, one day, God would be able to reconcile the hearts that were breaking today.

Fighting back tears, I told my dad I would see him in nine months. I can still see his face as we hugged goodbye and he walked away. Have you ever felt like you couldn't carry the cross that had just been dropped on your shoulder?

Then we had emotional goodbyes with Bryan's family. Bryan's younger sister, Rebekah, and her husband of two months had also come to see us off. That was tough for Aimee; she was especially close to her aunty. Bryan's parents were due to come to America that February and stay a week with us. They would be en route to California to help Elizabeth with wedding plans. That was only four months away, so it softened the pain of that goodbye. We knew we would see them in May, as Elizabeth and Daniel had set their wedding date for May 11.

November 15, 2011

We arrived in Denver.

Bryan had arranged a rental car for a couple of weeks. Once our house money came through, we would buy a car. Also, due to all the stuff we had (two children, two dogs, eight suitcases [one dedicated to Jonathan's asthma medication], a mountain bike, and a set of golf clubs), our new landlord was kind enough to meet us at the airport with his truck. Thank God he did; otherwise, we wouldn't have made it to Colorado Springs, which is about eighty-five miles from Denver International Airport (DIA).

It was dark when we arrived. Our landlords were very sweet. They had put basics in the house and mattresses on the floors. They said we could give them back once we had beds. As we came through the doors, I said, "Well, kids, this is your new home. Dogs, this is your new yard."

We all decided to try to sleep. The next day we would need to shop.

Bryan and I were up early, so we said to the children we would venture out to find more supplies. Top of the list—a kettle so we could make a proper cup of tea! With directions from our landlord, we found Walmart. We were so surprised that Americans could buy guns at a grocery store. *This place is very strange!*

A Healing Testimony: Faith like a Child

Over the next couple of days, we settled into our new home. We went out and ordered necessary furniture and started to explore the area. One morning I said to Jonathan, "Are you taking your inhaler?"

"No, Mum. God told me I won't need my medication in America! I don't need that anymore. I feel great! I can breathe okay!"

Colorado Springs is at a far higher altitude than England, so the air is thinner. As I stood there staring at him as he carried on getting himself a drink, the Lord gave me a flashback to the day I was standing in the pharmacy.

"Faith like a child is all it takes, Sue."

"Wow, God."

To this day, Jonathan has never had another inhaler or steroid tablet! He plays soccer and is a healthy young man. He never doubted what he heard.

What follows is my journey through the first and second years at Charis. You will see how my heart changed as I became immersed in the Word and learned to grow in my trust of God. As I share my mountains and valleys, you may need to give me grace! But as I said at the beginning of this book, it's a journey and an honest portrayal of how I found my identity in Christ.

Chapter 13

A First Year's Journey Begins

November 28, 2011

There I was on my first day as a first-year November Charis Bible College student. I must confess that it seemed very strange being a student that day, especially when I was usually on the teacher side of the classroom!

Once I pushed past my sense of change, everything was going well. We were meeting some nice people. Vicki, from Canada, was one of them. It turnd out she lived down the road from us in some apartments.

The Lessons were good and interesting. It seemed I was primarily learning to navigate myself around the Bible. Bryan seemed to know a lot more than me. When a scripture was called, he could turn to it rather quickly. He seemed to know if something was from the Old or New Testament. Here was another side of himself he somehow kept from me over the last eighteen years that we'd known one another.

It was quite a task getting used to the area. Bryan was driving everywhere. The roads are big and wide, all about three lanes. This kind of a road would be a motorway (freeway) in England! But all the roads seemed to be like that here, not just the freeways.

I was already missing family loads. Despite my emotions, I tried to look brave on Skype for their sake. At least the dogs seemed happy with their new garden, or yard, as the Americans like to say.

The first few weeks were a bit of a blur. Starting in November, we only had three weeks of college before taking three weeks off for Christmas break. I was not looking forward to my first Christmas away from England!

We were still waiting for our house deal to close. I had some time in prayer. I felt the Lord show me Psalm 31—the Lord is my rock.

On December 14, I had a call from my mum. My dear Great Aunt Audie in Wales has been taken into hospital. Aunt Audie had a very special place in my heart, so it was hard not to be there supporting my family.

Aimee was struggling with settling in at school at CSCS. Jonathan seemed okay, but I kept telling myself it's just the early days for us all.

Aunt Audie took a turn for the worst. I felt so far away from my family.

I spent some prayer time asking the Lord, *Why did this have to happen now?* Also, I told Him I had to have an idea that Audie would be in heaven. She talked about God, but I never really asked if she had ever asked Jesus into her life. I would have described her as spiritual, but she was one who never had any time for religion.

While after praying, the Lord showed me a vision of Jesus standing in the hospital room with her. Also, my nana was there, Audie's sister. My nana was smiling, and Jesus had His hand stretched out towards Audie. I also had a sense of peace. It was hard, but I felt Jesus say, "Release her, Sue."

Aunt Audie passed away.

I was **not** feeling in the Christmas mood! The family was still working things out for a funeral—looked like it would be in January, due to the Christmas holidays in England. I was trying to not be too down for Aimee and Jonathan, but I could see they were both struggling with not being in England at Christmas. Plus, we still had no news on the house. Mr. P.A. had seemed to have disappeared, supposedly back to America. I really hoped he came back with the money this time; ours was running out! What with setting up the house, putting a deposit on a car, paying for Aimee and Jonathan's school, rent on the house here, and the mortgage in England, there was not a lot left! HAPPY CHRISTMAS!

On Christmas Eve we, hadn't found a church yet, so we went to Woodmen Valley Chapel. Overall, it was a nice service, but it brought home feelings of not having family or really knowing anybody here. Vicki went to Australia to be with her son. Her husband had died only a year earlier from cancer, and she was on a mission to understand healing.

At least we had something to look forward to. Elizabeth was coming to us from Bethel for New

Year's. Elizabeth and Daniel had been in America since September and were planning their wedding for May. It would be especially nice for Aimee, as we planned to go bridesmaid dress shopping.

Christmas Day, we spent most of our time on Skype with family. All of us were crying, and of course, they are asking us questions about the house sale.

Elizabeth arrived, December 29, and everyone seemed happy to see each other. She had been a great support to us, as she was on a similar journey.

We had a successful trip to find a bridesmaid dress. The plan was for us to go to Bethel for about four days in May for the wedding. We also worked out a cake design too.

I was making their wedding cake, so I needed to find out how to travel to California with a wedding cake. We might decide to drive; I wasn't not sure yet. Our friend from the Vineyard church, Mike Millar, was going to come and stay and travel out with us.

January 6, 2012

Aunty Audie's funeral was today. I was unable to be there with our family. I was feeling very down that day. I kept asking the question, "Lord, what are we learning through all this?" Also, I had learned I had to have a tooth pulled as I had a root canal go wrong. It would cost us $500. I couldn't believe the cost over here. It's only been seven weeks, but I wanted to go home!

We tried New Life Church. It was a massive place: about 7,000 people. I've never seen a church that big in England. Aimee enjoyed the worship, and Jonathan enjoyed the children's area. I wasn't sure how easy it would be to get into a fellowship group with a church this size, but we were told they do have home groups. I did recognize some people from college there.

I was finding it hard to worship at that moment. I was so worried about spending money or lacking it. Maybe we should have waited for the house transaction to close before we came out. We were beginning to wonder about this Mr. P.A. Bryan was checking in with the lawyers in the morning. Nothing much happens over Christmas, due to the holidays. That's okay, but the bills don't stop coming in!

Finally, we were back to college. It was nice to see people again. Vicki was back from her trip to Australia to see her son and family. She had a good time. It was hard for her to celebrate Christmas without her husband.

Good news on the house—maybe that Friday the money wouldl be in place. Maybe I should take back all my unchristian thoughts about Mr. P.A.!

Wow, God, this is going to be tight. Bryan told me we only have $300 left in our American bank account. All our money was now tied up in our house. *PLEASE, PLEASE, GOD! COME THROUGH AND GET THIS HOUSE SALE COMPLETED!*

Bryan's parents were due out for a week in February. They were coming here after they had visited Elizabeth at Bethel to sort out some wedding arrangements. We were looking forward to seeing them.

We were on such a humbling journey. Bryan had to ask his family for some money until the house sale was completed. We needed a vehicle. We put a $1,000 deposit down on a truck. We figured we needed a four-wheel-drive with the Colorado weather! They would let us pay the balance when our money comes through from the house sale. I was just amazed that we had begun living like this—day to day.

During praise and worship time at college, I started thinking, *What happens if our residence doesn't sell? How do we get ourselves back?* It's true we had return flights booked for July, but not for the dogs. Watching Bryan seem totally engaged in praise and worship made me feel even worse!

Then in class, I was trying to focus. I was listening to Charis Bible College's founder, Andrew Wommack, teach *Harnessing Your Emotions*. Sorry, Andrew, but mine were all over the place at the moment. After the bell rang, Vicki asked if we wanted dinner-and-movie night in the week. *Bless her, I thought, she is taking me under her wing. I'm just feeling sorry for myself. What is it Andrew says? …Oh yes, I'm throwing a "pity party!"*

Another week passed with no closure on our sale! *What about money, God?*

Mr P.A. had gone to ground, it seemsed...

January 24, 2012 – *Toffee Apples*

We had been living on a budget, trying to work out the food and how to spend the last money we had.

This was crazy. We had twice as much outgoing as we did at that time the year before, but with NO income! I felt bitterness begin to creep in—not good. Why couldn't Bryan have done this in Walsall?

We headed to King Soopers, a supermarket, to get some shopping done. I was working out how many meals I could get out of a tray of chicken. *Maybe we should fast; we might hear from God!* (In those days, I didn't realize He is always speaking. If there was any problem, it was that we just weren't listening!)

Aimee and Jonathan ran up to us and asked, "Mum, we found toffee apples. Can we have them? Please, please! We haven't had a treat for ages."

Well, that broke us. I looked at Bryan as the heat of tears filled my eyes. *We can't even afford to buy our children a toffee apple.* He could tell what I was thinking. His eyes glazed over with tears too. There we were, in the middle of King Soopers, feeling like a couple of failures.

Bryan looked at the cost—four dollars each! Wow, we only had thirteen dollars for the entire food shopping.

"Okay," Bryan said, "put them in."

I just stared. *Okay, chicken and toffee apples it is.* I was so angry with him and God, I just had to walk off! The last few years, I had never had to think about how much I was spending on the food shopping. It never crossed my mind. Money was just always in the bank.

Five minutes later, Aimee and Jonathan came back to us. "We've had a chat with each other; we don't need those toffee apples."

They took them out the basket and placed them back on the shelf. This really broke Bryan.

Both Bryan and I left King Soopers in floods of tears that day. I could tell Bryan was dealing with some stuff.

When we got in, I went straight up to the bedroom and shut the door. Bryan had a face-on-the-carpet time with the Lord... *What's going on, God! You've brought us here and I can't buy my kids a toffee apple?*

After a few minutes of complaining to God, a scripture and a voice came to Bryan: 1 Timothy 5:8 KJV "But if any provide not for his own, and specially for those of his own house, he hath denied the faith, and is worse than an infidel."

Yes, God, I can't supply for my household... But God kept repeating the scripture to him. Eventually on the third time, Bryan heard the words, "Son, if I can't supply your needs, then My Word is void!" This, for Bryan, was a huge moment. It was a humbling experience, but something broke. Bryan knew at that moment that God would supply his needs. God was his Provider; it wasn't dependent on what Bryan could do. However, it took a while longer for my penny to drop!

The next morning, when we went into college, in our student mailbox was an envelope with our names on it. Inside was $200. No note, just cash.

Bryan and I worked out that, without the house sale, we would probably need $30,000 to get us through to the end of the school year: house rent, a car, living expenses, the children's school tuition, plus the UK mortgage and bills.

Mum and Dad wanted to Skype me. That, time I told myself, *Sue, don't cry. It's hard for them, plus they are worried that we have made a bad mistake*. In truth, I was asking the same questions on the inside too.

I was in shock after the Skype call with my parents. They had news: my Aunty Audie had left me some money in her will. This was a surprise, as three years earlier she had given me some money. She had said, "You have it now and enjoy it. I want to know what you do with it while I'm here."

I had discussed a couple of things with her, including wanting to send Aimee and Jonathan to the private Christian school in Trowbridge. She had thought it was good to invest in their education, so that's what I did until we came out to America. She had given the same to my sister. So, when Mum said that there's more for me, I was surprised. It turned out there was around 20,000 pounds! *Wow, I can't believe that. I can go home!*

I struggled in that moment because that was exactly what I wanted to do. I could easily have gotten my job back. My boss had said to let her know if I ever wanted to return. Bryan... Well, Bryan could do anything. It even crossed my mind, *Should I even tell him about the money?* All these thoughts were running through my head.

THEN God spoke. I hadn't heard much from Him for a few weeks (I wonder why!).

"Sue, all are called, but few are chosen."

Really? What does that mean?

"You are chosen for such a time as this."

Why is it once you have the Holy Spirit inside of you, your life isn't your own anymore? I asked myself.

After going back and forth with God and myself, I finally told Bryan about the money. He was highly relieved. The money from his family was running low.

We told Mum and Dad that once it came through, to transfer the money into our account. It would take about six weeks, they thought. Bryan and I agreed to try to finish the first year of Bible college at least.

The Second Gift of Provision

Over the next few weeks, Bryan and I discussed how we could budget out the 20,000 pounds till the end of the current school year. I know it sounds as if it were a lot of money, but with expenses for a family of four in one country and a property with a mortgage in another, it was going to be very tight for us.

My heart and emotions were still all over the place. I was reading through the Bible as is required during the first year at Charis. I really found myself in the story of God's people in the wilderness. The Israelites were moaning and complaining, why God had taken them from Egypt to the so-called Promised Land. I knew just how they felt! At home, I often said to the children and Bryan, "I want to go back to Egypt," meaning England was in my heart. However, Bryan looked at America as his Promised Land because of the call of God. So, when I looked at Bryan, I was aware of his tunnel vision to complete what God had called us to do.

I had to admit, though, along this journey, God was putting the right people into our path. It was remarkable to me how we were growing in fellowship and support with the other Charis students. In the past, back when Bryan and I weren't walking with the

Lord, our friendships were geared to having a good time, usually involving alcohol. So, getting to know students on a similar journey was quite different for us.

We kept quiet about our situation except to a close group of Charis friends. We didn't want people to know we were struggling. But this group was very strong, and later in this book, you'll see how that same group is now all over the world doing great things for the Lord.

Two of our closest friends, Vicki and Lisa, would pray for me, as I was the other half of the couple who obviously needed it! They would continue to give me the same scriptures over and over: Proverbs 3:5-6 and Jeremiah 29:11. I struggled to stand on the reality of trusting and believing that He had a purpose for me at all times. But now these verses are foundational to my journey. **If you don't trust Him, how can He work in your life?**

Earlier in January, we were in need of a vehicle. We put a down payment on a Ford Explorer, and the dealership had agreed, in consideration that we had a house sale pending, to allow us to drive it off the lot. We updated them weekly on the progress of the house sale—or not! As each week passed, they grew more nervous, until finally, after six weeks, they uncomfortably told us, "Please return the car." To our amazement, they returned our down payment of $1,000. We then had to rent a car weekly until the sale of the house was completed.

Bryan's parents came to visit. They were coming for a week, as they were also traveling to California to see Elizabeth. She and Daniel were planning to get married on May 11. We were praying and planning that we would be able to go. It would break my heart if I couldn't. But May was a long time off; surely the house would be sold by then.

We had a good week with Bryan's parents. They were looking at our circumstances carefully, wondering if we were okay. They had been very supportive. Bryan's mother had struggled with her decision to introduce Bryan to Charis in Walsall in March 2011. She never imagined we'd all end up in America. Even back then, I could see restoration on the horizon between Bryan and his parents.

They blessed us with groceries while they were here. These were all hard lessons for Bryan, I could tell. After being in control for all those years in business, this was a humbling season, having to accept help from his parents or from any other channel the Lord chose to use.

As first-year Charis students, everyone has to do service hours. Bryan had started to go to Dan Funkhouser's church. He was helping Pastor Dan transition into a new building. For my service hours, I worked in the Watering Hole, a small cafe on the Charis campus, washing up dishes after the lunchtime. At least I felt I was doing something. Not being able to work was killing me. I had always worked, apart from a couple of years when the children were babies. How much easier it would be for us if internationals were permitted to work! But due to immigration laws, we couldn't. Maybe God had forgotten that!

Charis was going well. We were now prayer ministers at Charis's Thursday Healing School. I didn't know then how much Healing School would be a big part of our journey at Charis. I really enjoyed praying for others; it took my mind off myself. I would listen to instructors and the Healing School coordinators and think, "Wow, what great faith."

A Charis instructor, Greg Mohr, was teaching on the fruits of the Spirit. I thought, *This would really be a great course if he could leave out the section on patience!* When the instructor started to teach on it, God audibly said to me, "Are you listening?"

"No! Not really what I want to hear."

But the Greg's words were like a spear in my heart. I had to get my head around this. I was being consumed with the house sale, with what we didn't have, and with what life had been like before. Satan was having his way with my emotions. I didn't like Andrew's teaching on *Harnessing Your Emotions* either. I can remember thinking, *Well, you don't know my situation.* Only later would I learn how very self-centered it was of me.

Then one day, a fellow student came up and gave me Andrew Wommack's book on self-centeredness! Can you believe it? However, when I eventually decided to read it, about 6 months later, I thought, *Wow, thank You, Jesus. I did need that!*

We were facing having to give up yet another rental car this week. In first period worship, I was crying out to God—actually crying!

"Don't you know we need a car?"

And don't ask where Mr. P.A. had gone!

My emotions were made worse by all the singing people around me who looked so happy. Bryan leaned over and said, "I know this is tough for you, but God's got this, Sue. You just have to trust Him."

I remember thinking, *Well, is He going to pluck a car out of the sky for us?* As worship ended and we were walking back to our seats, a lady came up to me and said, "This may sound a bit weird, but do you and Bryan have a car?"

I just stared at her. "Sorry?"

"Well, during worship, the Lord told me you needed a car. And you see, I purchased a new car a few months ago. God told me not to trade in my old car, that I would be giving it to someone. Well, I've been at Charis nearly four months, and today He said to offer the car to you two."

"YES...YES, we need a car!" Then, of course, I burst into tears and blurted out that we were having to give our rental car back that day because our house hadn't sold. She said we would talk at long break.

I went and found Bryan. When I told him, he teared up and said, "I told you God had a plan."

Well, this dear lady gave us her car, a 1998 Nissan Pathfinder. It was immaculate and had only 190,000 miles on the clock, and it was a great gift. She told us to come and pick it up on Saturday.

God Working

When I saw the car's plate, I just stared at the numbers: 777. It was white, and God had shown me, in a dream about six weeks before, the four of us in a white car. I didn't know then what He was telling me. I shared my dream with my family, and they said it was a real God setup. The Pathfinder proved to be a faithful car for us. Both Aimee and Jonathan learned to drive in it.

During March, Beth, the dean of women, came up to us and asked if we would like to join the student care team. She said we had a gift to help, especially internationals, and she felt Bryan could develop this area. This was an honor to be asked. It was a perfect opportunity for Bryan to excel at a challenge, and it would help keep my mind off the sale of our house in England. On that, there was still no news. We had now remarketed the house and brought the price down. God only knows where Mr. P.A. had gone to!

March 26, 2012 – Aimee's 15th Birthday

This was the first family birthday in the US without our extended family. As Aimee opened her cards from England, the tears rolled down her cheeks. I couldn't help but cry with her. My heart still ached for England and especially our family.

We received an email from Mr. P.A. saying he had no idea now when he could purchase our house. *Wow!* I felt so deceived from this man, all his false promises, and where was GOD in all this?

Oh well, maybe we can scrape through to the end of term and then go home. Bryan was far less negative than me. He said, "God will come through. Remember He called us here for three years, and God told me we would be debt free after the third year."

To this, I thought, *Three years? I'm just focused on getting through the next three months!*

Back at college after spring break, Beth, the dean of women came up and said she had another assignment for Bryan and me. I think she was trying to take us under her wing and stop me from giving up!

So, Beth's mission for us was to host a single mum from England with her son, David, who had the condition of autism. Beth thought we were best suited to host her for two weeks, since I used to work with children with special needs—and they were English, of course!

We picked up Ola and her son from the airport and took them straight to college, as Healing School was on with Carlie and Daniel. Healing School was the best place to start; Carlie prayed for David, and Daniel and Bryan spoke with Ola. It was Easter weekend, so there was no school the next day, as it was Good Friday.

When we brought Ola and David home to our house, we introduced them to Aimee and Jonathan. Jonathan immediately took David under his wing and got out his Hot Wheels cars for him to play with. Jonathan has always had an empathetic nature; he enjoyed helping me out at preschool with the special-needs children back home.

We took them around to the shops the next day. It amazed me how we, as humans, have to explore our environment whenever we go places. For us, it was the American shops. Ola wanted to make the most of her time at college listening to Andrew. So, Beth arranged permission for me to stay at home with David and pick up on my course work later. David was only eight years old, so he was not allowed in the classes, except for Healing School and praise and worship time.

Ola wanted to go to Pastor Lawson Perdue's church because she had seen him on television. It was a great service, and again Ola went up for prayer. Jonathan took David into children's church. Ola was prayed for and received the baptism of the Holy Spirit. She had a lot of questions that afternoon. I thought, *Wow, she's asking me, and I'm just learning about all this myself!* But Bryan, as usual, seemed to have a handle on it.

We went off to college Monday and left Ola and David to explore the neighborhood. Aimee asked, "Mum, is it okay to leave people in the house you don't know, or is this our life now?"

I look back over our three years as students at Charis, and I really have to give honor to my children. Not only had we taken them out of their country and away from family and friends, but they had also radically adapted to their new lives. I thank God that they are the most amazing young adults now. God, by His grace, blessed them and gave them the ability to walk this journey with us.

On Tuesday and Wednesday, Ola went to college with Bryan, and I stayed with David. Then we all went to Healing School again on Thursday.

Ola would ask if we could get more prayer for David, but we said, "You can, but he has already been prayed for. Now you have to stand and believe what has already been taught."

Ola was also enjoying the instructors' teaching on healing. She said how she would love to go to Charis herself, but we all knew what a commitment and sacrifice that would be for a single mum. I told her that Charis in Walsall (UK) was a place where she could get plugged in. She lived in London, about a three-hour drive away.

David also suffered with asthma, so we shared the story of Jonathan's healing from asthma. I thought David seemed calmer after prayer at Healing School. Ola asked how she would know if he was healed.

"When you believe in your heart and confess with your mouth," we told her.

"Knowing" is the revelation you receive once you believe and stand on the word of God, even if you don't see it in the natural. It's a bit like salvation; you may not see anything, but believing what you confess has changed you.

The next day, I suggested we drop Bryan and Ola off at college, so I could take David to Focus on the Family, whose headquarters are located in Colorado Springs. As I was getting ready to go, David said, "Miss Sue, I can't breathe. My chest is tight."

I calmly said, "David, you are okay."

"No, I'm having an attack, Miss Sue."

I went and got his puffer and quietly prayed over him, but I could feel his body tensing up. I knew what to do in the natural, as my own son would have asthma attacks in England. But I felt this was a spiritual attack. I thought, *No, Devil. I'm taking David to Focus on the Family!* So, I prayed and started to read healing scriptures over him. Then he started to read them with me. I felt a great peace come over me. I think that was the first time that I really heard the Holy Spirit instruct me when I was praying for someone.

About thirty minutes passed, and then David said, "I'm good. Can we go now?"

We had a great time at Focus on the Family. For those of you who don't know, there is a huge slide there. David went up and down this slide for about two hours, not once struggling to catch his breath!

On their last weekend with us before we took them back to the airport, Ola wanted to go shopping for wigs! This was a new experience for me. Bryan found a few wig shops in the Springs. David and Jonathan had their last trip to the park and then to McDonald's before Ola and David flew back to England. I believe she did receive understanding on healing, and so did David. I also think David, just like his namesake, will be an amazing, godly man and bring many people to Christ. I know God has a great plan for him.

Charis Worship Conference

The Charis Worship Conference was a new event and an opportunity to earn mission points, which would go towards our required second-year mission trip. We served as ushers. During the first session, one of the security guards, who was also a classmate, came up to me.

"Hey, Sue. There's a really sweet lady here from England."

"Of course, all us ladies from England are sweet!"

"Would you like to meet her at the break?" He then added, "I think she could do with some help from you and Bryan."

We met Anuli; little did I know this would be the start of a sweet friendship. She was a beautiful lady, so full of the joy of the Lord. She had two walking sticks with her. I asked what she needed them for. Anuli said she had multiple sclerosis. So, I asked if she was here for healing. She said, "No, I've come because I want to be a worship leader or sing in a worship group."

Wow, I thought, *I'll never again assume to know what people want!*

After the conference, we asked her where she was staying. It turned out she was in the Hyatt hotel at the end of our road. She had arranged for a cab to pick her up and drive her to and from the conference. We offered to take her back, rather than her having to pay for a cab, and then we also invited her to dinner with us.

So, we brought her back, and we took care of her over that weekend with meals. The following year, she managed to get up to Grace and Faith in Walsall, UK. There she met my mum and dad and spent some time with them.

On one of my trips back to England, I was able to go and visit her in Hastings, Kent, with my parents and pray with her. She lives with a care nurse these days but has the most amazing faith. She now and again will send me words of encouragement.

I think that month of April changed me. It helped me to put my focus onto other people rather than focusing on my stuff not working out the way I thought!

JUST STAND

PART 2

Learning to Walk

Chapter 14

ELIZABETH AND DANIEL'S WEDDING DAY

May 11, 2012

Bryan and Aimee went to California for Elizabeth and Daniel's wedding. For Jonathan and me, the day began with calling Aunty Elizabeth and Uncle Daniel to wish them our love and that everybody would have a nice day. At least Bryan could go to support his family and Aimee was a bridesmaid to Elizabeth. I was happy that Bryan could spend a few days with his family. Even though we only had enough money for two people to travel there, I now know that I really should have stood in faith for finances for us to go as a family together. That was the main lesson I would learn of this journey. Don't trust what you see in the natural—expect the supernatural!

Although we were both in America and just a few states away, it was impossible for us to just pop over and see them for the day. In England, you would just drive somewhere. You could get to Scotland in a few hours, but not here. The landscape is so vast.

Late in the day, Jonathan asked if he could have a couple of friends over for a sleepover. I think the thought of spending the night with me wasn't high on his to-do list!

My friend Vicki invited me to a gathering at the home of some of our college friends. I thought going would be good for Jonathan as well, as they had two boys the same age. We had a good time of prayer and fellowship together as Charis students. We all shared our prayer requests. My request, of course, was for our house sale to go through. *Gosh*, I thought, *this is getting so boring. I hate talking about it. We have been in America for six months now.* Someone said to me that maybe God wanted to provide for our time here and that we only needed to rest in that. *There's a thought … but I'm guessing my thinking can't understand that concept!*

Monday came and brought with it me having to drive back to Denver to pick up Bryan, Aimee, and Mike. (Mike was a close friend from our Vineyard church in England.) Mike was heading back to the UK on Wednesday. *I would give anything to go back with him,* I thought. *But I can't. I have a family here. I can't just run away.*

Jonathan headed off to his sixth-grade mountain camp for three days. He was excited to be with his friends. Meanwhile, Bryan and I sat down and worked out the numbers. We had enough money to carry us to the end of July.

We already had flights booked. The children were flying back three weeks before us. They finished school the end of May, and we booked their flights for June 29. As we were November students, Bryan and I had to do summer school to cover the course work from the first trimester, that we had missed. It was okay for us to go to school in the morning. Elkton was only five minutes away from where we lived. But after June 29, we would start our volunteer hours for the Summer Family Bible Conference, where we would be working in the children's ministry all week. Then we had another couple of weeks until we were due to fly back, around July 15. Bryan kept saying we would be okay; God would come through by the summer.

The bottom line was we needed $30,000 to come back for the second year. It was required to be in our bank account to complete the M-1 student visa, since we couldn't work in the US. We not only had all the outgoing expenses that we had established in the US, but we also had a mortgage and other expenses going out of our English bank account. So, juggling finances on both sides of the pond wasn't fun. To my surprise, in spite of our difficulties since coming to America, I could see God answering some of our prayers. We were definitely becoming closer as a family.

We had one low offer come through on our English home, for 75,000 pounds less than the asking price. Bryan said, "We can't take that—plus we don't know if it's just a try-on."

As I've said before, selling a house in England is very different from selling a house in the US. So, Bryan felt a phone call to Mr. P.A. wouldn't be amiss. After we reached out, we got an answer in twenty minutes from him via email. He still wanted the Barn, but he was waiting on the deal to come through on his home before he could purchase ours. He planned to be in England in August to complete the deal. THANK YOU, JESUS! That was what we had been waiting for.

For the end of Spring term Promotion Breakfast, we all headed off to the very nice Antlers Hotel in downtown Colorado Springs. It was strange for us, as November students, that everyone walked across the stage to collect their completion of first-year certificate. However, as November students, we just got a handshake to seal our intent to finish! We almost felt like losers for not being here in September! Perhaps that was me just being cynical. It was a nice event, and if you had asked Jonathan, he thought the crispy bacon was the best!

Provision Three

The next testimony just goes to show that despite how we are thinking about things, God can shake us to your roots with His faithfulness. Have you ever felt like Jonah hiding in the belly of the whale? That was me!

The friend who had given us the car was also in summer school with us. One day she asked, "So, how are you fixed with your finances? My husband and I have been praying for you."

"Thanks," I said. "Well, our buyer is back on the scene, so we are hoping to go back to England and finally complete the sale on our house."

"So," she asked, "do you both believe you will be back here in September?"

"Well," I said, "That's the plan. Bryan said God called us for three years."

Her response really caught us off guard:

"Well, my husband and I have been praying and we felt God wanted us to give you this check."

She handed me a check for $5,000. I just stared at the check as the tears started to roll down my cheek.

"It's a gift to you both," she began, "to help you get through the summer and get back here in September."

This was another humbling moment. *Why would God tell someone to do that when I spend most of my time moaning? God, whatever it is in us that You see, I thank You for Your faithfulness.* So, we thanked them very much. They said it was all part of sowing and reaping, which was what God had shown them.

On Sunday, after going to church at Heartbeat Ministries (Dan Funkhouser's church), we met Vicki for a nice walk around Ute Valley Park.

We told her about the gift. She just smiled, saying, "Well, God's given you a little more, hasn't He?"

I sensed she was quietly familiar with the path we found ourselves on. Later that day, I prayed, "God, give me a thankful heart. Not just because we have received this gift, but because I can trust You. Lord, I feel as if I've been on a roller-coaster of emotions the last seven months. I need to focus on one thing. What one thing can I focus on?"

Suddenly, I felt His presence around me. The words in my head were, "What's on your heart, Sue? What do you want me to show you?"

I just spoke out loud, "Show me how to love like You do."

Well, I knew that response had bubbled up from my spirit. If my flesh had answered the Lord, I know it would have said something very different for sure!

No sooner had the words left my mouth, I began to wonder, *What do they mean?* Then I asked, "What scripture do you want me to meditate on?"

"John 3:16," I sensed Him say.

Of course, I thought: *For God so loved the world that He gave His only begotten Son, that whoever believes in Him should not perish but have everlasting life.* (John 3:16, NKJV)

We had Monday and Tuesday off from college, as summer school didn't start until Wednesday. The children were still at school, so Bryan and I had time to sit, read, and pray together. I shared with Bryan my experience in God's presence and the scripture He had shared with me. Bryan looked relieved. The expression on his face seemed to say, *She's finally getting it.* However, he didn't have the courage to say that!

I responded anyway, "I know what you are thinking. I'm trying not to live in the flesh, but it's hard, okay!"

"Okay," he said. "Let's pray together in unity. God can show us how to love like He does."

So, we did.

Later in the day, there was a knock at the door. A lady stood there. She was there to sell us windows.

As soon as she started her sales pitch, I interrupted her, "I'm sorry, we aren't interested. We rent; it's not our house."

"Okay," she said, "but it's so hot out here. Can I use your restroom? I've been drinking so much water today."

"Yes," I said and showed her the restroom.

Bryan was sitting and reading on the couch. It was so hot for Colorado. It was up in the 90s. It was as if we were having a heatwave.

As she came down the stairs, she asked, "Where are you from?"

"England," I responded.

She said, "Oh, are you military?"

That was everyone's question around the shops.

"No," we answered, "we are over here studying at Bible college."

"Oh, wow," she said—and took a seat at our table! I looked at Bryan and he just smiled, so I asked, "Would you like some water?

Well, I thought, *she is obviously going to ask some more questions.* We were used to that from the shops.

She said, "I've been praying to meet some Christians today. To be honest, my life has been a mess. This job is just a start for me. I've been in rehab. I was in a prostitution-and-drugs gang in Denver."

Well, I looked at Bryan as I put the water down in front of her. Then the verse John 3:16 came into my head, followed by His words; *For God so loved the world that He gave His only begotten Son, that whoever believes in Him should not perish but have everlasting life.* (John 3:16, NKJV)

She explained the details of her colorful life on the streets of Denver. I could feel my flesh react a bit, especially when she said, "Sometimes these rich guys would turn up—you know the ones where their wives didn't understand them or give them what they needed."

But as this woman talked, I had this involuntary wave of compassion come over me. I could see that Bryan was already gearing up to talk about salvation.

Then I said, "Would you like some watermelon?"

"Very profound, Sue!" I heard the Lord say to me. "Just love her like I love her. I don't see her sins."

Thankfully, Bryan began to steer the conversation to ministry and how Jesus valued her. He explained all she had to do was receive His love.

She responded, "How could God love and forgive me?"

In that moment, it was like Bryan and I were somehow joined in unity to minister to this woman to whom we had opened our door.

We explained that God doesn't look at our sins. He was aware of all our sins, and because of His love for all of humankind, He paid for them on the cross. We explained that is what He looks at if we are wanting to give up that life and turn to Him.

"Simply accept Him as your Lord and Savior," I told her. "God loves you so much that He wants the best for you. He's not judging you. He's just standing with His arms open waiting for you."

The kitchen was full of His presence. I could feel it as we were leading this lady to the Lord. We ministered and chatted with her for about an hour and a half. After two cups of tea and a bowl of watermelon, Diana accepted Jesus as her Lord and Savior. She received the complete package as we also led her into the baptism of the Holy Spirit. She started speaking in tongues straightaway. We didn't send her away empty-handed either. We gave her CD recordings from Charis instructors. Some of the CDs were by Duane Sheriff, while others were of worship music. Finally, on her way out the door, she asked if she could have our phone number, so we gave her the landline number. (Truthfully, I was a little uneasy about that).

Bryan went outside to give her another book, but she had disappeared!

As I reflected on it later that evening, I realized what an amazing couple of hours Bryan and I had had. We looked at each other and agreed that was pretty cool.

"You know, Bryan, she never gave us any sales materials about the windows!"

"Yes, that was strange," Bryan said. "I have been reading Hebrews 13:2, (NIV) 'Do not forget to show hospitality to strangers, for by so doing some people have shown hospitality to angels without knowing it.'"

We haven't heard from Diana again, but I know that was a life-changing experience. The only question is, who was changed more—her or us?

Later, when I had the opportunity, I asked my neighbors if a woman had knocked on their doors to sell windows. They all responded that no one had knocked on their doors.

One thing God had shown me after that experience was that our strength would be in ministering in unity together as a couple. Of course, there were times when I questioned that. Inwardly I told the Lord, *No, maybe Bryan should be the only one on stage—not me. I can't see that, Lord!*

First week down of Charis Bible College's summer school, seven weeks to go. There was a long time ahead of us of watching various instructors on DVDs. At least the Discipleship Evangelism course is done in groups, which was fun.

Aimee and Jonathan finished school for the summer. Aimee was really struggling; she'd made friends but still missed England so much, as do I. It wouldn't be long now for her—just three weeks until she would be home for a summer break.

One day Bryan and I were prayer ministers at Healing School. An older man came up in a lot of pain with a trapped nerve in his back. Bryan and I both laid our hands on him, and I felt electricity go down my arm into his back. As we prayed, I also saw a picture of a little man chipping off cement from around a brick. After we finished praying, he bent down, saying the pain was gone. He started to praise Jesus. I shared the picture of the little man chipping away, and he said he had arthritis.

I said, "Well, that's gone now too!" *You go, Sue. Bold as a lion,* I thought.

He shared that he had been to the doctor's last week, and the doctor had showed him his hipbone covered with arthritis.

He said, "I believe that has gone now, after the vision you had."

"That's cool," I said.

God said to me as we were clearing down from healing school,

"So, do you want more visions?"

"Oh yes, please," I said. "I like pictures."

So, He gave me this scripture to meditate *on,* James 4:7-8 (NKJV).

> *Therefore submit to God. Resist the devil and he will flee from you. Draw near to God and He will draw near to you.*

The one thing I liked about summer school was the smaller number of people. We were really connecting, especially as we were building towards the big Summer Family Bible Conference. This was the biggest of the four conferences that Andrew had at that time in Colorado. So, in the mornings we had college, then in the afternoons, we would be at Vicki's apartment pool or Chris and Lisa's apartment pool. This was especially great for the kids as the weather was so hot and we had no air conditioning! It was Colorado's hottest summer on record. There were a few forest fires around, but not near us—praise the Lord!

We were focusing on college and just believing that everything would sort itself out once we were back in

England. We had four weeks scheduled back home, and I couldn't wait.

Everything was falling into place. We found a student, Rebecca, at college who was willing to house- and dog-sit. We had to make these arrangements because we had found out that we could not travel with the dogs on the plane during the summer months. Plus, Bryan said, "It cost me 2,000 pounds to bring them here, and I'm not paying to take them back!"

We had told our landlord we had to go back to complete on the sale of our house. He was okay with Rebecca staying, and we promised to be back by August 15. The children were due back to school by then. We knew we needed four weeks to get up to London to sort out visas, but none of that could happen without the completion of our house sale.

I was also noticing how things were changing with our family. Both sets of parents, even though they were born again and spirit filled, were heartbroken about us leaving the UK. To soften their sense of separation, we would share with them teaching on what we were learning. It turned out that Barry Bennett was my mum's favorite teacher! I could see how God was moving in our families, even though not everybody was on our page. However, after these last eight months, they likely were amazed at what we had managed to do. Bryan would have long chats with his mum, which was something of a new thing.

We received an email from Mr. P.A. He communicated that he was just waiting on some paperwork from the lawyers and that he should be ready to sign contracts on August 1. THANK YOU, JESUS! PRAYERS ANSWERED.

We celebrated with our friends from school. The drama of the last eight months would soon be over. It was August 2011 that Mr. P.A. first saw the house and said he wanted it. I never thought it would take a year!

Saturday, June 23, 2012 – Waldo Canyon Fire

We all decided we would have a day out at the Royal Gorge, a local canyon and tourist attraction: Chris and Lisa, Vicki, me, Bryan, Aimee, and Jonathan. As we headed out, it was such a hot day. Strangely it was even hotter in Colorado Springs than it was farther south! Despite the heat, it was good fun. However, we were all melting by the end of the day. Vicki suggested that we stop for a dip in her pool on the way back.

However, as we were driving back, Chris and Lisa got a call from their neighbor to say that the fire that was in Waldo Canyon, just west of Colorado Springs had changed direction and was heading towards the city. Lisa and Chris were concerned about the smoke in their area; they lived so close to that side of town. We suggested that they stay with us for the night, so they headed off to pick up some things for an overnight stay, along with Smokie, their cat.

The next day Chris and Lisa decided to stay with their friends Mitch and Susan. Unlike us, they had air conditioning—very wise. Plus, we had arranged for Rebecca to move in so she could get used to the house and dogs before we left.

As part of summer school, we still had to do our service hours. That meant Bryan and I continued serving at the homeless center downtown. As Bryan and I headed south toward the center, I said,

"Bryan, it's so smoky. Do you think we should leave the children at home?"

It had been forecasted that the fire would be going across the mountains, not towards the Springs. My question just hung in the air. We were both quiet, but I kept thinking, *I hope we are doing the right thing*.

We had only been at the homeless center for five minutes when Aimee rang: "You have to come back. They are evacuating the area. The fire has changed direction and is heading our way!"

I said to Bryan, "I knew we shouldn't have come"

Bryan said, "Me too."

"Then why did we?" I asked.

"Sue, just get in the car," he said.

I prayed in tongues all the way back, while Bryan was on the phone with Aimee instructing her what to gather: "Get to the safe. You need to get the passports and the visa stuff. Pack up the dogs' stuff. We will be there soon."

As we turned onto our road, it was like a war zone. People were running around loading up cars. Bryan ran down to Mary Hershberger's house to help her with her six children.

"Where can we go?" Mary asked. She had no plan in place.

"We will go to Marilyn and Jack's house," we said. "They live across town on the other side of the interstate highway."

So, we called Marilyn. Chris and Lisa and Mitch and Susan were already there. Luckily, she had a very big house, so Mary and her kids were welcome.

We gathered our two children, the dogs, and an overnight bag. As we left the Rockrimmon area, plumes of black smoke rose and ash fell. Reports were already coming in that Mountain Shadows had been taken by the fire. That was where Pastor Dan and Penny Funkhouser's house was. I wondered if they were okay? We also knew of some students who were renting up there, as well as other friends from Heartbeat Ministries Church—Andrew and Jen.

It took us all of forty minutes to go five miles across town. I kept thinking that what I was witnessing looked like some scene from a film, but we were in it.

When we got to Marilyn's house, there were twenty-four of us in total, eight of whom were scared children, plus four dogs and three cats! But we were safe, and very grateful that night as we watched from the top of University Park as a wall of fire came down the mountain. We prayed for the wind to change direction and go back up into the canyon. But as you can imagine, the news coverage wasn't very positive. Already the fire had taken two lives and 400 properties, according to early estimates.

Bryan and I took charge of the kitchen and produced Spaghetti Bolognese for twenty-four people. Then the men sorted out air beds, and we all prayed together most of that night that the wind would change.

I said to Bryan, "We have to go back to the house. We forgot one piece of paperwork that the children need to fly back to England with."

As they were both still under sixteen, they would need British Airways assistance. We had three days until they were due to fly home. I said to Bryan,

"No matter what happens, they are not missing that flight!"

So, we agreed that, even though they had evacuated our area, we would try to go back and see if we could get the paperwork. Bryan decided that he would try to see if he could get in. Chris went with him. The officer they encountered said he thought they would open up our area the next day for residents to go back in.

The ministry decided to cancel Summer Family Bible Conference. So many people had lost their homes in the Springs that hotels were at a bursting point and couldn't handle out-of-town visitors. We were not sure what that meant for summer school, but I was more concerned with getting my children safely back to England.

Finally, everyone left Marilyn's house to head back to their own homes. Rebecca came with us to ours. Amazingly, our house didn't smell of smoke. The only place that any smoke could be detected was in the basement where a window was left open.

The Mountain Shadows area was still blocked off. It looked like some type of war zone. Houses were burnt down to their foundations, and twisted metal was strewn about everywhere.

We had twenty-four hours to pack everything up for the children to fly out to England. I was a little nervous as they would be flying without us. But I wanted them with their family. They had been through quite a lot over those nine months—well, those few years, to be honest. What great kids we have! Thank You, Jesus, for Aimee and Jonathan.

As we were driving up to Denver, Bryan got an email from Mr. P.A. All paperwork was still moving well and would be on time for August 1. Thank You, Lord. I really wanted to send the children off with some positive news.

The Denver airport was packed with people everywhere. When we got to the British Airways desk, the flight attendant asked if we would consider giving up the two flights for twenty-four hours. I said no because the children needed to see their grandparents. Well, her question triggered Bryan's years of being involved with the airline business.

Bryan stepped in. "What deal will you give us?"

Wow, a spark of the old Bryan coming back! He turned to me and said, "If they will give us a good deal, let me handle this!" So, I took the children to one side and said, "Dad may get a deal. Would you be okay in flying out tomorrow?"

They both looked at me, "Do we have to go back to the house?"

The Deal!

Bryan came back like a man who'd just struck gold.

"So, kids, this is the deal. If you give up your two seats tonight, they will put you on the same flight tomorrow night. We have a night in a hotel, food vouchers, and coupons for a Denver attraction tomorrow. What do you say?"

Excited, Jonathan asked, "Can we get burgers?"

Then Bryan turned to me and says, "I also secured $2,400 in air miles towards our flights back here."

I had to laugh. I only missed that old Bryan sometimes. I agreed and said I would let the grandparents know to hold off for twenty-four hours.

So, we left DIA, headed off to a restaurant, filled our bellies, and were off to the hotel. Thank God for Rebecca already being at the house. We texted her to let her know we would be back tomorrow night instead.

Bryan said to me, "See, Sue? If we trust Him, He will always come through. It may not have been as you imagined but He has our backs. With the money towards our flights back, He is already showing us that we will be back in September."

We had a great day the next day at the museum in Denver with the children. It had an IMAX cinema as well, not to mention the fact that it was the only place we had been to that had air conditioning. The temperatures were still really high. Later that evening, back we went to DIA, and the children flew off to England to be met by their grandparents.

The ministry decided that they would open up Elkton for a Fourth of July celebration for the students and anyone in the area who wanted to come. This would be our first Independence Day in America, so I wasn't really sure what to expect.

It began with a very patriotic evening of worship. It was great, but I cannot lie, dear reader: it did feel a little strange celebrating their independence from the UK! But I figured, we are all one family under Christ!

Due to the fire, we learned summer school would finish early that year. We finished off the last of the DVDs as we awaited our promotion from first to second year. Bryan was chosen to give the first-year speech. He felt honored but was a little nervous.

All that was left was to clear things out.

In my quiet time one morning, I asked God, "What have I learned this year? Apart from my whining and complaining?"

Almost immediately, I heard Proverbs 3:5-6, of course.

> Trust in the LORD with all your heart, And lean not on your own understanding; In all your ways acknowledge Him, And He shall direct your paths.

That last morning at school, as we cleared out our college stuff, I went to our mailbox to check on our last test results. There was an envelope with our names on it, and inside was $350. I had told the Lord that since school was wrapping up early, I wanted to move our flights in order to get back to England earlier. Bryan said it would cost $200 to change the flights and we weren't being good stewards if we changed them. With the envelope in hand, I showed Bryan. "Look, Bryan. God supplied the extra, so He wants us to change the flights!"

We changed our flights, and the $150 left, we contributed to the fire collection for the Springs.

When I had an alone moment with Jesus, later that night, I continued our conversation:

"Another thing I learned was it's great to receive, but it's also great to give. Sowing and reaping does work! As Pastor Dan, our pastor from Heartbeat Ministries, told us, 'If He can get it through you, He can get it to you. *In one hand, out the other, as it goes through, there's enough for you.'*"

Now, Dear Reader, if that gift was from you and you are reading this book, we want to thank you personally for your obedience to the Holy Spirit. As you continue reading, you will see that over the course of our time at Charis, God used many people to keep us on this journey. Some gifts, we knew who they were from, but other gifts came to us just like that. But God knows what you did, and you will be blessed back in this lifetime.

We met with Pastor Dan and Penny about serving in the church. They offered to mentor us when we got back from England. *Wow,* I thought, *not sure what that looks like, but we want to support them with the church for sure.* Dan is a different pastor to most I have come across. He and Penny just live Jesus. They have huge hearts for people and, for some reason, feel we were worth the investment! We agreed to meet when we got back at the end of August. We ended with a great time of prayer together, the four of us.

Before our summer travels, Bryan and I also had a meeting with Beth from college. She wanted to talk about creating an international committee. Building systems was something Bryan was working on during service hours with Beth. Sometimes the contrast between my experience and Bryan's was amazing. He was coming up with new committees for the college, and I was washing up in the college kitchen for my service hours! But everyone has to start somewhere.

I could also tell that Beth saw something different in Bryan. He put together a whole policy and procedure process for internationals coming to Charis. There wasn't really anything in place before we came. He compiled information that internationals would need when starting at Charis, like how to open US bank accounts, where to get furniture, good schools for their children to attend, and more. Some of Bryan's materials are still used today. Lisa and I helped the cause by collecting stuff, from yard sales. We had a double garage, so it was full of stuff. New people would come and get stuff and other people whom the Holy Spirit moved on would drop stuff off. A pretty cool system was up and running. Lisa loved meeting all the internationals; she had a heart for them. I said to her one day, "I bet God sends you overseas because you have such a heart for internationals!"

Then it came—the day I had been waiting for! We flew home to England. It'd been nine months since I had seen my family. I couldn't wait. *Hurry up, flight!*

You must be thinking, *Well, that was a tough year, but things look like they are turning around for the Nutmans*. Read on!

Chapter 15

BACK IN ENGLAND

We had some great times with family those six weeks. I just wanted to hug my mum and dad when I saw them. *Wow, how the nieces and my nephew have grown!* We spent time visiting friends in Trowbridge and went to see our old pastors. It was good to chat with friends. They were all very interested about what was going on. They also were still trying to understand why we felt we had to do this.

One day, I was able to meet with one of my dear friends, Jacquie, whom I had known since moving to Trowbridge. Jacquie and I had met when Aimee was two and her son George was about the same age. We both went to "baby gym." We had been through a lot together. She had gone through a divorce recently and had moved back to Bournemouth. Jonathan and her second son, Harry, were very close. I used to look after Harry when he was little. Jonathan and he were like brothers really.

We met in Sidmouth for fish and chips on the beach. She kept asking, "Why are you doing this?" I couldn't explain things to her satisfaction. Jacquie said, "Wow, I really thought you would end up like me, divorced, Sue. Now you and Bryan are at Bible college. I can't get my head around that. Bryan seems so different!"

I felt God really put her on my heart. I knew that He wanted Jacquie to know Him. But I wasn't brave enough to ask her!

> On a happy note: On a later visit to England, in November 2014, I led Jacquie in the salvation prayer. She is now a born-again, Spirit-filled believer and a very close friend. In 2019, on another trip back to England, Jacquie and I spent a day together. I had the pleasure of water baptizing her in the sea at Bournemouth.

It was had such a nice time with family and great days on the beach with my sister, Maddy, and her two children, Archie and Mabelle. We had been very close before Bryan and I had left for America, and I had also spent a lot of time helping to look after the children. Hence, we had all experienced heartbreak when I'd left; Mabelle was then four and Archie, six and a half.

Spending time with brothers and sisters was so special, as well as the time spent with our parents. We could see they were concerned about the situation. Bryan spent a lot of time with his parents, sorting through our storage and seeing what he could sell. He also chatted quite a bit with his brother, Colin.

Colin and his wife, Rachel, were supportive. They said they understood why we were doing what we were doing. As Aimee and Jonathan played with their cousin Lily in their garden, I can still remember Rachel saying, "I'm sure it will be okay, Sue, but whatever happens, you, Bryan, Aimee, and Jonathan are better off now for going through this than you were a few years ago."

I agreed. Rachel and I had always been close as sisters-in-law and have known each other for a good twenty years.

Aimee had a fun day out with Aunty Rebekah, Bryan's youngest sister. She took Aimee to her beauty salon, which was nice. These two were like peas in a pod! Everyone thought they looked and acted like sisters. So, those few weeks were precious to us for sure, even though we still had the house sale hanging over us!

We headed back to the Barn, our unsold estate, to check on things. The poor place looked unloved, to be honest. We had arranged for people to pop in and check on it, but Bryan and I spent a whole day cutting the grass and hedges and cleaning the place through. *There you go, all clean again, ready for your new owner.* Which, of course, was the topic on everyone's mind: Was the sale really going through now?

Mr. P.A. emailed Bryan to say he had to take a trip to Malaysia but would be back at the end of the month. No sale meant no tickets back to America. No sale meant no visas. Yes, we still had the house in Colorado Springs, where our two dogs were being cared for, but by this time, Rebecca had to move out as her own place was available. The four weeks she had agreed to stay turned into six weeks. But everything was okay; Lisa found a couple from India with a little boy. They had come in to join Charis, but they had nowhere to stay. So, Lisa put them up in our house and told them about feeding the dogs. She kept an eye on things there as well. But the big question on both side of the pond was, were we coming back?

We decided to change agents, which turned into a discussion that maybe renters would work better in the Barn than trying to sell it. But the issue was that the rent alone would only cover the English bills. What about America? We had gone through all our savings, my inheritance, and the money that family had lent us. I said to Bryan, "This is crazy; we can't carry on. What shall we do?"

Making it worse, both our extended family and our children were worried about us, which was completely understandable. Plus, the great faith I had in America was fading fast.

Bryan and I went through all our stuff. Bryan got out his Breitling watch, worth a few thousand pounds, and a personalized license plate, "BAN 1", and put them both on eBay to sell.

"That will cover August here and September in America," he said. *Wow,* I thought, *we are being completely stripped.*

We were living out of suitcases in our parents' home. *What are we doing?* We had to tell our US landlord about the situation, so Bryan called the landlord who, as you can imagine, wasn't happy. Bryan said he would fly back and sort everything out. It was our only option. I FaceTimed Lisa, and she said that the Indian family had found a home but that she was keeping an eye on the dogs. I couldn't stop crying. This was a nightmare.

Regarding Mr. P.A. Was he a complete con man? Who would want to do this to a family?

Reality Check

Bryan decided to take the airfare mileage credits from June and fly back to sort out the US house and fly the dogs back. I emailed my boss, and she said I could go back to my old job. I was sure the children could go back to Emmaus, even if I didn't know how we would pay for that either. *What a mess, Lord. Have we missed You?* I had so many questions in my head. I could hardly think straight. Our children thought we were mad; what a year we had put them through. I cried out to God: *I JUST WANT STABILITY FOR MY CHILDREN!*

I hadn't been able to hear much from God over the previous few weeks. But as Bryan headed off to catch a plane back to America, I prayed, *"Lord, what are we to do? My children are heading into important educational years. You called us for three years to be trained for what? This mess we are in now?"*

I kept reading Jeremiah 29:11-12 and Proverbs 3: 5-6. "This is Your Word, Lord, but it's not working in our lives!"

As Bryan left, he emailed the dean of students, to ask when the latest we could all return was. "The tenth of September" was his reply. *Well, we need a miracle*, I thought. It was so hard saying goodbye to Bryan at Heathrow. How different things had seemed nine months earlier. As the children and I drove away from Heathrow, Aimee said, "We all should be on that flight, Mum, not just Dad!"

We knew all our friends were praying for us in the US, but from here in England, things didn't look too great. I had brought Andrew Wommack's book, *The Believer's Authority*, home with me, and I felt lead to read it the night Bryan left. As I read the book, words would jump off the page to me. I was transfixed; I couldn't put it down. I was staying at my parents' house, and Aimee and Jonathan climbed into bed with me. We read the book together. As we read it, I felt something rise up inside of me.

"This is wrong. What's happening to us! We should be blessed; we are following God's plan," I told the children.

"Okay, tomorrow we need a day out, a field trip."

"What?" they said.

"Well, you both have work from school to do, yes?"

Their school in Colorado, Colorado Springs Christian School, had already started two weeks earlier. I was having the school email work over for Aimee and Jonathan.

"I don't know how, but we are going back to America." Wow, for the first time ever, I felt like I wanted to go back!

So, the next day, off we went on our field trip, armed with my *Believer's Authority*. We headed to Escot for the day, a stately home with an educational center. We had a fun day together, just the three of us. Jonathan wanted to do the mud tunnel, which meant crawling on his belly in mud! Oh, joy—my mum was going to love Jonathan when he got back.

Poor Bryan had a horrible flight back to Colorado. There was a five-hour delay in Chicago, but he finally got back to the house in Colorado Springs.

Back in England, I was looking through some of my stuff that night, and I found my prophetic training notes from a course I had taken at Bath City Church. Fiona, a close church friend, and Bryan and I had gone to this training course with. I was a bit skeptical at first as this prophetic stuff was all new to me. But the six-week course changed how I would hear from God. As I read over my notes, I realized that I understood them more than I had a year ago. What really encouraged me were the words I was given at the time.

Suddenly, the words in *Believer's Authority* were real and just for me. I said to the children, "I feel God wants us to pray in tongues together,"

Aimee said, "Yes, you as well, Jonathan."

"I can't," he said. So, Aimee and I prayed for Jonathan to receive his spiritual language, and he did start to speak in tongues. We all prayed together, and I said, "We can expect good news from Dad in the morning!" I'm not sure where that came from, but I was believing.

I just kept reading over the words given to me previous October in Bath.

Remember, dear reader, these are the words and pictures people had given me!

- My timing – not yours
- Being able to change and adapt into a new role
- God is your provider – Jehovah Jireh
- Let God provide – shared finances

- Always enough
- Time of release is coming
- Trust and wait

These were the words people had given me along with the pictures of eagles, mountains, planes on runways, and an American flag. (Remember, none of the people at that training knew where we were heading.)

As I read those words, I realized in my heart that all year my focus had been on the house sale and not on God's plan for our lives.

"Lord, I repent, and I know You have a good plan for us. I know You love us, so it's going to be OK. You've got this, and whatever it looks like, I trust You!"

Across the Pond

In Colorado, it was already the end of the first week of college. Bryan had to chat and pray with Dan and Penny. He also went in to see the dean of students. They, as well as our classmates, were all praying for us.

Two of our classmates invited Bryan over to dinner; they felt they had something to share with him. Basically, they felt God was telling them to bring us back to America because we hadn't finished our assignment yet. Bryan tried to explain that this was not a small sum of money! We needed a minimum of $30,000 straightaway to get visas, plus living expenses until the Barn sold (and by now we had reduced the price in hopes of a quick sale). But this couple was sure they had heard from God. They understood about the house, and they believed that by sowing into us,

God would sow back to them an investment property. Bryan, of course, said he would need to pray about this, chat with me, and seek wise counsel. We weren't just talking about a few hundred dollars here!

Bryan felt led this morning to go to New Life Church in Colorado Springs. He just woke up and God said to go there. He had been praying in the night, asking if we should accept this couple's offer of help or not. God confirmed it to him. The pastor was talking about how Lydia in the Bible supported Paul. Bryan clearly heard the words, "THEY ARE YOUR LYDIA" (Acts 16).

Bryan next spoke with Pastors Dan and Penny and the Charis instructors. They all felt that if the couple was sure they had heard from God and was willing to sponsor us as a family, maybe this was God's plan. But they all left the final decision down to us to accept the offer of help. Bryan had to verify with the Dean of Students whether we could still make it back in time.

"Well, it's really too late, Bryan. How long will it take you to get your visa?"

Bryan replied, "A week!" Which in reality was a joke, as the wait time for an interview was at least three weeks in London. I had already checked into that.

The dean of students said, "I don't know why, but we will give you until September 19 to get back here."

Bryan rang me to let me know all the details.

"The money is being transferred over tomorrow. So, I need you, Sue, to book up and arrange the visa interview. You will have to try Belfast in Northern Ireland, as we know London has a three-week wait time. Right now, remember we need an appointment this week, Friday at the latest. I can get a flight out of here on Wednesday; you will need to pick me up in Heathrow Thursday. Friday really is our only option for an interview if we are going to get back into the US next Wednesday."

"That's only a week away!" I said.

"I know, Sue. If God's in this, it will happen."

I relayed this to my parents, who were standing in the kitchen with their mouths open!

"Well, how will all this work out?" my dad asked.

"I don't know, Dad, but we just have to try."

The next day, I called Belfast to set an appointment. I was told there were only two appointments available, both for after September 22. *Well, that's no good,* I thought. *We need to be in America by the nineteenth.* I was told that the only thing we could do was to put our names down for a cancellation.

"Yes, please," I said.

I got off the phone and said to the children, "Well we need to pray. In the name of Jesus, we believe and claim we will get a cancellation appointment on Friday, and our visas will go through by the time we leave next week. Plus Lord, we need it in the middle of the day so we can fly in and out of Belfast the same day!"

Mum and Dad just looked at me. I said, "That's how we pray; we **take** our authority!"

Within an hour, I got an email from the Belfast embassy with an appointment on Friday at *12 noon*! I could hardly believe it; we were all jumping around in the kitchen.

Then Jonathan said, "Mum, I had a dream that I would be standing in our kitchen in America, pointing at the calendar, saying, 'See, we are here by the nineteenth.'"

"That's right, Jonathan. You are right. God's got this!" I said.

I must admit, I was quite shocked to get an email from the embassy that quickly. I texted Bryan in America to tell him.

"Okay, great, Sue, but now you need to book flights from Bristol to Belfast. Remember to allow enough time for the appointment. We only needed three flights, since Jonathan doesn't need to come because he's under fourteen." (Plus, after the first rejection, Jonathan wasn't keen on embassies).

The next forty-eight hours were crazy. Bryan left Lisa in charge of the house and dogs. He arrived back to Devon on Thursday evening, and we were up at 4 a.m., driving to Bristol to catch the flight to Belfast.

As the three of us sat in the embassy's waiting room, I said to Bryan, "What about proof of Aimee's flight back? We have our driving licenses, but how can she fly back without her passport?"

This was a real concern since the embassy keeps your passport as they have to put the new visas in them.

"Well," Bryan began, "they will give Aimee a letter giving her permission to fly back without her passport."

As we sat there waiting, people were coming out from their interviews complaining. "What a waste of time. Don't expect to get anything from this place," one guy said. Another bloke, too angry to speak, kicked the chairs as he walked past us. We just quietly sat there and prayed in the Spirit.

A young, redheaded Irish girl opened the door and, looking at us, said, "The Consulate will see you now."

As we entered into the interview area, Bryan spied Aimee's permission letter sitting on the Consulate's desk. The interview began with a few questions: Were we planning on coming back?

"Yes," I said, "we want to open up a Charis Bible extension school in Devon." (Sue's idea again!)

Then the interviewer turned to Aimee and said, "And I guess when you get back to Colorado, you'll be learning to drive because you're fifteen?" Aimee nodded. To this, the Consulate replied, "Well, I'm granting you the visa for your second year at Bible college. When you come back again to apply for your third year, we would like more information on the third year schools."

"Okay!" we said. "THANK YOU!" We were trying not to leap up and down in the Consulate's presence.

Once outside of the embassy, we said to each other, "Wow! That was the easiest interview yet."

We quickly went to pick up the paperwork from the Collecting Office. There we were informed that we needed a specially sized envelope from the post office, so they could mail the passports back to us in England. After we had run around Belfast to find the post office, we picked up the envelope and legged it back to the embassy, all against the clock. This was all happening as we were running to catch our plane back to Bristol. What a crazy treasure hunt!

As we delivered the required envelope at the embassy, we asked when we could expect the passports to arrive. They casually responded,

"Possibly next Thursday."

"Oh, no!" we protested. "That's too late for us to get back to Colorado."

To which the clerk said, "You're in the hands of the mail system."

But we knew we were in the hands of God because the dean of students had said that the latest we could return was Wednesday, September 19.

With God nothing will be impossible (Luke 1:37, NKJV).

As we drove back to Devon from Bristol, it was already midnight. Once back at my parents' house, I laid my head on the pillow, and I heard the Lord say, "**Book the flights**!" To which I responded, "Oh no—not again, Lord."

I woke up the next morning and told Bryan that I felt God had said to book the flights. He just laughed nervously. I said, "We must be so crazy."

"Well," Bryan said, "let's see what flights are available next week."

The reality was that we needed to be back in Colorado by September 19! Jonathan was quite sure in his dream that God had shown him he would be standing in our kitchen on that date. As we checked the flights, they were all coming up booked apart from Tuesday, September the 18. The next flight after the eighteenth wouldn't be until Saturday, September 22, which was too late to get back and start Charis. We were in so deep now that we could do nothing else but book these flights and trust God that the passports would arrive.

Much to the horror of my parents, we broke the news that we had booked flights. I tried to reassure them by telling them what happened with the Belfast appointment. But even I agreed, we sounded crazy!

We were all packed and ready to leave, anticipating Mum and Dad's post arriving around lunchtime. We had to leave by 2 p.m. to catch our plane back to Colorado. The post came—nothing. There were no passports. This was a real test of our faith. We needed to trust and believe in supernatural faith. Twenty minutes later, a bike courier knocked on the door. He handed us a padded envelope. Our passports had turned up!

A courier or an angel—who knows? But against all odds, we were heading back to Colorado for our second year!

Chapter 16

SECOND YEAR

Vicki came and picked us up from the airport. Chris and Lisa were at the house with a cup of tea waiting for us. The dogs went crazy (bless them); we had been gone a total of nine weeks!

Jonathan stood at our kitchen calendar and said, "See, I'm here pointing at this—just like in my dream."

The next day, we entered the second-year classroom at Charis. Pastor Dan interrupted his teaching and said, "Praise the Lord! The Nutmans have returned," as only Dan would!

Wow! Second year seems different. I noticed some familiar classmates were missing, and there were about forty new people from correspondence and other extension schools.

On break, I began to realize that the main topic among the students this year was which mission trip they would be going on. Trip assignments were being posted on Friday in the breakroom. The missions coordinator had already emailed Bryan and me in England, as we had missed filling out the trip preference forms during the first week of school.

Students made their top three preferences known, but the missions department traditionally chose what trips students were assigned. Bryan said he felt God had told him he was going to Columbia. I thought I would be going to India, as I imagined myself with little brown-skinned children. Finally, on Friday, we checked the board with everyone else. Bryan was on the Columbian trip; he smiled smugly. *I thought, quit proving you're more spiritual.* As I searched for my name, I found it under Ecuador. *Okay again, Mr. Nutman. It doesn't mean you are more spiritual than me!*

Most of October flew by. We had the Ministers' Conference, where we worked as hard as we could for mission points. Mission points were used as credits towards the cost of the mission trips. Because there had been no Summer Family Bible Conference due to the Waldo Canyon fire, we were going to be behind in mission points. Bryan and I served wherever we could to accumulate points for our second-year trips. I served in the green room on the hospitality team; Bryan was on parking duty. We also ushered and did prayer ministry when we could.

The children settled back into Colorado Springs Christian School. The school had been excellent again this school year with helping us with their tuition. What a God-given school that was for our children.

Back on the English home front, we had to lower the price on the Barn. The housing market in the UK had really slowed down. We discussed this with our sponsors and explained the situation. It was so hard not knowing when things would sort themselves back out. I felt the Lord say the house would sell in 2013. To which I responded, "Lord, I pray that it's in January!"

I didn't like the idea of having to ask every month for another check from the couple who had decided to sponsor us. Bryan said we needed to focus on what we were here for.

"Keep your eyes fixed on God, Sue."

Almost weekly I would seek counsel and comfort from Beth the dean of women. It always involved a lot of tears on my behalf. She would say, "Sue, you have to learn to rest in Him, precious one."

People in our class began to know about our situation. This meant we were regularly asked if our property had sold.

Even Mr. Andrew Wommack asked us, "Have you guys sold your house yet?"

"No."

"Well, pray and believe it's done!"

"Yes, Andrew. That's what we are doing!"

Healing School on the Road

One of the things Bryan and I loved to do at Charis was serve at Healing School. We were there every Thursday. We got to know Daniel Amstutz and Carlie Terradez and worked closely with them. My confidence in praying for people was really growing.

Healing School had only just started the year we joined Charis, so it was in its second year, just like us. Daniel and Carlie were talking to the prayer ministers about taking Healing School on the road. They were taking a team of students to Kansas. Carlie asked us if we were able to travel together since our children were in school. *How exciting! A road trip*. Lisa offered to stay and look after Aimee and Jonathan. It would only be for two nights.

It was a week later that off we went. We loaded the Charis shuttle bus with instruments, product, and AV equipment. We were all juggling many roles on this trip: prayer ministers, product setup, cashiers, and ushers, as well as setup and teardown crew— what fun. I think, looking back, this was one of the turning points for me. God really spoke to me on this trip: eleven hours in a minibus, you need to focus on something!

We had over 500 people turn up. The students from Charis Kansas City also helped at the event. Daniel and Carlie taught. The whole room came forward for prayer! People got their sight back, deaf ears were healed, legs grew out, and tumors disappeared! I did feel a little overwhelmed at first, and then God clearly told me, "Just love them through My eyes. I will heal them!"

After hearing from God, it was easy then. I just had to realize that when praying for people, it's not about ME!

As we drove back from Kansas, I kept thinking, *What a privilege this time was.* I was thanking God for allowing us to go. *I want more of this*, I thought. When Bryan and I had the chance to minister together, it felt good and right, a bit like the time when the mysterious Diana turned up to sell windows.

Staring out of the window at the endless flat fields of Kansas, I felt the Lord take me back to the word He gave me about Bryan and the two of us ministering together. I suddenly saw us together teaching on a large stage. *That's amazing*, I thought, while I was simultaneously stressed about the thought of standing in front of people to speak!

Then He took me back to what I would call the dark years of our marriage. On the outside, we looked okay, but we were far apart. Unfortunately, this was when the children were very little. Bryan was off chasing business, and I had the children as my world. When children are young, I think those years are very tough on a couple. Who Bryan and I were growing into being now was a stark contrast to who we were in those years. In the back of my mind, I knew there was a day coming when we would have to walk through some difficult terrain from our pasts in order to get to the future that God had for us.

November 14, 2012

A Charis instructor, Greg Mohr, had been teaching on family in one of our second-year classes. He laid out the principle of how the family and relationships should be.

1. GOD
2. SPOUSE
3. CHILDREN
4. MINISTRY

He was talking about how we need to get our priorities right before we go into ministry.

Wow—I now get it. God has to come first, but my other areas are completely out of order.

He went on to explain in a marriage, there needs to be two people. But if they have two different focuses, then it's not long before the devil gets into the relationship to have his way. Bryan and I were both so caught up in our own worlds that our different focuses had put a wedge between us. I suddenly realized, once that happened, we opened the door to a lot of stuff that wasn't good.

As I was thinking about this, God dropped a scripture into my head, John 10:10 (NKJV):

The thief does not come except to steal, and to kill, and to destroy. I have come that they may have life, and that they may have it more abundantly.

I finally felt I was getting heart-revelation knowledge. The Scriptures were coming alive to me. I can see where they were fitting into my life, and God was slowly taking me on a heart journey with Him. Surprisingly, I was beginning to look at Bryan differently too. *Wow, we have only been married twenty-one years!*

Bryan was always happy to serve around the college. He seemed to have this natural ability to give these profound words to people that would usually make them cry! In a good way, if you know what I mean.

Fellow students often said to me, "Wow, Bryan's knowledge of the Word is amazing; he ministers so well." Which was usually followed by, "Was he always like that?"

"No!" I would respond, hesitating over how much to share, "My husband has had a Saul-to-Paul conversion. I would say on the *road to America,* not Damascus!"

But I was happy for him.

Bryan and our friend Vicki were chosen to go with a group of other students to work at the Dallas Gospel Truth Seminar (GTS). I was so pleased for him. Seven international students were coming in for winter term. Bless them; that was us last year. Lisa and I were ready to help where we could. We had a couple over for dinner, winter term international students. It was kind of cool going over everything with them.

Bryan was returned from the Dallas GTS. He had an awesome time. A few days from then would be Thanksgiving! A fellow student was holding a big party for sixty students, including the new internationals. Everyone brought a dish to share; it was a great time of fellowship. Standing on the balcony of my friend's property, I couldn't believe that we only had two-and-a-half weeks left of Fall term.

And still no house sale.

Christmas 2012

I was excited for this Christmas. All second-year students now knew where they were going on their mission trips. Mission team meetings were increasing in weekly frequency. The first team had come back from the Dominican Republic. I was due to go in March, Bryan in April. We did separate trips so that one of us would be able to stay at home with the children. I was actually looking forward to going on the trip by myself. It would give me a chance to see how God would use me without Bryan always going first.

Daniel and Elizabeth were coming to stay for Christmas. Daniel worked at Bethel School of Supernatural Ministry, and Elizabeth was a second-year student at BSSM. They had been married for seven months now, so we had family with us for Christmas—YAY!

Christmas Day was great. We Skyped with both families, and Chris and Lisa came over for dinner. We all watched the Queen's speech. Chris and Lisa were very excited because they were off to England, Ireland, and Scotland for their mission trip. We missed Vicki on Christmas Day, as she had gone to Australia to see her son and daughter-in-law. Vicki would be going to Columbia with Bryan.

Back on the English home front, we also had good news on the Barn. The house had a viewing. Our dear neighbor Tony was showing this couple round. The news came back that they liked it.

"I just want it sold, Lord. I'm so grateful for the support and sponsorship, but I'd really like to get this burden off of us."

I just felt like we were living in debt the whole time, and that's not God's plan for us! I would get into panic when I thought that we were going to Bible school on other people's money. Yet, even in the midst of this, I was beginning to harness my emotions better; Andrew would be pleased!

New Year's Eve 2012

We had a party at our house for our student friends; a couple had just gotten engaged. We opened it up for our entire class, and it ended up that about seventy people came. Thankfully, everyone brought something to eat. It almost felt like the old life in England—but without the copious amounts of alcohol. Actually, it was quite nice not to have a hangover on New Year's Day! We ended the evening by making a number of people watch the fireworks from London on the computer.

Bryan had done so well on the Dallas GTS that he was chosen again and was now off to Phoenix. They were beginning to take students to help, as the conferences were getting bigger.

Daniel and Elizabeth were heading back to Redding, California, so I took them up to Denver for their flight.

We had an email from the agents selling the Barn. The couple liked it, but it was out of their price range unless we came down another 50,000 pounds. Then, strangely enough, Bryan had another email from Mr. P.A., seeing if our house was still available. WHAT! Is he playing a mind game?

We asked if the couple could go up any more, but they said they couldn't. The agents also felt that they would send more people to view the property soon. Then another option made its way to us: our other neighbor's son wanted to rent it with his wife for three months. We accepted that. At least someone would be living in it. And it would give us some breathing space and help with the mortgage.

Of course, we had to tell our sponsors all of this. They agreed we shouldn't let it go for a silly price, but I could tell things were getting tense between us.

Furthermore, between not being at school for another five days and being by myself, my mind wasn't doing me any favors. I tuned into a teaching by Joyce Meyer on patience—boy, did I need that!

"Patience is not the ability to wait. Waiting is a fact of life. Patience is the ability to keep a good attitude while you are waiting!"

I need to get my head back in the Word, I thought.

I was working on my next assigned small group message and trying to get my nerves in order. The thought of speaking in front of my fellow classmates, as well as a supervising third-year student, terrified me.

Back to college. Worship was great, and the teaching from the Charis instructors was inspiring and challenging. *Yes, I will put on my big girl pants and be brave!*

God gave me a great scripture in worship: Be not dismayed for I am your God; I will strengthen you (Sue). Yes, I will help you with My righteous right hand (Isa 41:10).

Back on the English home front: Tony's couple from Christmas came back with a slightly higher offer. But they wanted us to pay all their legal fees? Our lawyer bill was already high due the infamous Mr. P.A.! We had a chat with a few people, and after seeking wise counsel, and even though this went against everything we were learning about being blessed, we felt we needed to move forward with this couple. I knew God would repay all that we were losing in this lifetime!

> And everyone who has given up houses or brothers or sisters or father or mother or children or property, for my sake, will receive a hundred times as much in return and will inherit eternal life (Matthew 19:29, NKJV).

The Barn sale was agreed to—THANK YOU, JESUS. We were so happy to tell our sponsors. We could start to work out the deal to pay them back the sponsors. They now indicated that the sponsorship was a loan. I didn't feel comfortable having their money anyway; that's not how Bryan and I work. I think in the beginning they were okay, but as the months wore on, they were getting nervous, understandably. I'm sure initially they thought that the sponsorship would only last for a couple of months. But after six months in, I could understand their anxiety. With the price of the Barn going down so much, all I wanted to do was graduate from second year in May.

I had been spending a lot of time in Hebrews 11.

> The fundamental fact of existence is that this trust in God, this faith, is a firm foundation under everything that makes life worth living. It's our handle on what we can't see. The act of faith is what distinguished our ancestors, set them above the crowd. "Heb 11:1, The Message"

Money or Peace?

In Philippians 4:11, it tells us to be content with whatever we have. One thing Bryan and I had learned was to not focus on money. Funny that when you don't have any, nothing to focus on!

In our old lives, money wasn't an issue. I had access to whatever I needed; the checkbook was always available. However, in Colorado, we counted every cent and were learning how to give on top of that as well. How does that work? The Kingdom of Heaven principles were at work. In our old lives it was, "get what you can; keep it all to yourself." But now it was "Give first, and there will be enough left for you!"

If money guaranteed happiness, wouldn't the rich be the happiest people on this planet? I was reading the following devotion, and I thought it was quite profound: *As I looked around, the man in front of me had seemed to have had it all—money, freedom, friends and family. But he didn't have the one thing he wanted most—happiness. His home life would horrify most people: his kids were alienated from him, his wife resented his obsession with work and he allowed himself no time to kick back! But what was this man's biggest concern? Keeping what he had! Maybe you are reading this thinking "I could be happy in his situation." No. Money can't buy you happiness; regardless of how much you have, it's never enough! Fear will always whisper "unless you get more, you won't be secure." So what's the answer to happiness?*

> *Paul wrote in Philippians 4:11-13, "For I have learned to be content with whatever I have – I know how to live on almost nothing or everything. I have learned the secret of living in every situation, whether it is with a full stomach or empty, with plenty or with little. For I can do everything through Christ who gives me strength"* (UCB Word for Today).

As I read this, I realized, this really was our journey, and what was written was us before B.C. (before Christ)! You see, when you pursue God, or God pursues you, God's purpose for your life is primary, and money is secondary. Your real status symbols are salvation, spiritual growth, a secure home, family, friends, and the satisfaction of doing what God has called you to do.

As I was meditating on this, I heard God say to me, *"The glory is not in the money. Glory is in the faith you have to follow Me."*

I felt God speaking to me through this battle, despite what was happening in the natural. God then gave me the scripture in Romans 4:20-22 (NKJV). Again, He encouraged me to *believe and just stand*.

> *He [Sue] did not waver at the promise of God through unbelief, but was strengthened in faith, giving glory to God, and being fully convinced that what He had promised He was able to perform. And therefore, "it was accounted to him for righteousness."*

Interns for Third Year

When they came into the second-year classroom to present internships for third year, we had a form to mark off our top three choices. One couple, Mike and Caroline, were the current Healing School interns. As they were talking about their internship, I heard that familiar audible voice say, "You and Bryan will be Healing School interns next year!"

I looked around to see if someone was standing behind me.

"Well, God," I quipped back, "if you want us to do that, we need that house sale to go through!" As if He didn't realize.

After the class, Carlie Terradez asked Bryan and me, "Are you back for third year?"

"That's the plan," Bryan piped up.

"Well, I think you both should apply for the Healing School internship," Carlie said, "You both would be great."

When we got home, I told Bryan what I had heard, so we put it down as our first choice.

Then another shock. Our sponsors told us that month would be the last they could support us, and they wanted to know how soon we could pay them back. It would be as soon as our property was sold. We really were grateful for what they had done, standing in the gap for us, but my thoughts went into free fall *"Jesus, keep my heart pure, please."* I kept wishing we hadn't come back last September.

It was a very tense time, as you can imagine. I had so many questions and tears.

"God, I can't believe we felt You said this was the right thing to do. I hate that we are in so much debt now. If I had known this last September, we would never have come back for second year."

After all my tears and the shouting to God, I clearly heard Him say this to me: "Sue, I'm not in charge of people's free will."

I think this was one of the most profound things He had said to me. So, I began to think about all the things God puts into place but we fail to follow through on because of our free will. That's very freeing if you think about it.

This was a tough time, especially being so near to my mission trip. Bryan met with the couple and said they would get every single cent back as soon as the house sold. They agreed to wait but said that they couldn't give us any more money. I can totally see where they were coming from. They had already given more than they probably first thought. Also, when God tells you to do something, you need huge trust, especially when it involves money. I think both parties had learned from this. God clearly told Bryan and me just to bless our brothers and sisters in Christ and don't get offended. Really, how could we? Without them, we wouldn't still be here! We were learning more lessons on this journey, and Proverbs 3:5-6 came back to mind again.

We had enough money left for one month.

Our dear friend Vicki came around to see how the meeting had gone between Bryan and the sponsors.

"Well," she said, in her Canadian way, "I've been on this journey with you guys, and I know one thing for sure. You will walk that stage in May and graduate! I will give you enough money until the end of May. Then you can pay me back once the Barn is finally sold."

We wrote up an agreement and signed it. She organized the funds and said that no one needed know; it's just between us. As you can imagine, there were more tears from me. As one door closed, God opened up another one.

Provision Four

I had to get my head around the fact of owing more money. There were only a couple of people who knew what we were dealing with. I didn't stand on the chairs shouting about what we were going through. Chris and Lisa were supportive and great encouragers. Many a worship time, I would be having a pity party, and Lisa would lean over and whisper to me, "Give Him Praise!"

I was excited for them, as they were leaving tomorrow for England on their mission trip. I gave her a list of things to return with: salad cream and tea bags, please.

As the student body was praying over them like we did with all the mission trips, I had my hand on Chris, and the words just came out: "You're going home, Chris." He looked at me.

"Wow, I don't know where that came from. I'm sure it doesn't mean heaven!" I said to him. "God is really going to speak to you both over there." I knew they would have a great time; they were such great encouragers.

Bryan was going to Columbia in April, and Vicki was on his trip, so she came round a lot as they were both leads on the trip. I knew God had placed her in my life. She was like a spiritual mother to me.

Ecuador – My Mission Trip

I was so excited to go: just me and God. Well, there were, of course, ten other people and our mission leads. I had been put over all the children's ministry, due to my experience in England. It was planned that we would have three full days with the children's church group, plus a trip to an orphanage. I packed a load of activities and lesson plans in my case.

The trip ended up changing my life. I think because it was just me, I had to trust God. I loved the teaching bit and sharing of our testimonies. Of course, people loved to hear how we came to America. I really felt like I was doing God's work. I began to realize how important it was to put into practice what we had been learning. We taught in churches and in a drug rehabilitation center for men. The two guys on our team had to be the teachers there, as it was a cultural thing. But we had about twenty guys give their lives to Jesus and get baptized in the Holy Spirit. They were going down like flies!

We had a couple of fun days at a banana plantation and also took a boat ride around the port. There we ministered to the fishermen. I wasn't looking forward to that because of the smell of fish!

So, I prayed, "Jesus, tonight I want to minister, but I don't want to smell the fish!" To tell the honest truth, the only thing I could smell all that night was the sweet smell of lilies! And there were buckets of fish everywhere.

I loved the children's church. Maybe it was because I was leading it? I think it was because I just did what I used to do back in England, and it flowed. We translated some of the songs I used to sing, and they worked great. Do you remember the vision I had about my mission trip in first year? God showed me little brown-skinned children, and I thought that it meant India. But as I sat on the floor with all these children around me, I looked at their skin, and it was brown. They looked like the children in my vision! *Wow, God, that vision was from You!*

This trip was only nine days long, but it changed my life. There is a world out there waiting for someone to say YES to God.

Black Day!

We got an email from our lawyers. The second buyers had pulled out from the Barn sale, the week before we were due to exchange contracts.

What were we going to tell our sponsors? We met with Vicki. She said, "Well, they will just have to wait— like me. I promised to get you to graduation, and I will. Anyway, I still believe you are both meant to do third year. I'm doing third year, and I'd like you two to be there as well."

Vicki, Chris, Lisa, Bryan, and I had all decided we wanted to do Third Year Ministry School under Greg Mohr.

We had guaranteed we would pay back all the money we owed once the Barn sold. God told us the Barn was to be sold. He also told us we would be debt-free after the three years at Charis. We had to stand on that promise.

We readvertised the house. At least with spring coming up, the weather would be nice. It was a beautiful place in the summer. Plus, we told the couple renting it that they could stay as long as they liked, but they were moving to Australia in about five weeks.

There were only eight weeks now to graduation. Bryan was again chosen as the class speaker. *Wow, what an honor for him. Glad it wasn't me!*

Aimee's 16th Birthday

As you can imagine, some of our close church family were on this journey with us. Andrew and Jen, from church, had become very close friends. They had a little girl, named Teagan, whom I would help babysit. I was chatting with Jen one day when she asked about what we were doing for Aimee's sixteenth Birthday.

"Not a lot" I said, "with the ongoing current financial situation." Jen said, "Well, Andrew and I have been praying, and we want to bless you as a family. It's spring break; we want you to go away somewhere, the four of you, and celebrate Aimee's sweet sixteen birthday. It's a big thing in America!"

"Wow, what a blessing." Yes, I was crying again.

We had a family chat and decided on a road trip to the Grand Canyon in Arizona. We booked a hotel for two nights with a pool, and off we went with grateful hearts. Aimee was blown away that Jen and Andrew would do this for us. The plan was for her to celebrate her sixteenth birthday at the Grand Canyon. As we were preparing to go down there... Oh yes, our truck decided the day before we left to break down! So, we had to get it to a garage. Another friend lent us his truck instead. It was a proper truck, a Toyota Tundra, so Jonathan thought it was his birthday too. The friend would pick up our truck from the garage after it was repaired.

As we were heading down the road to Arizona, suddenly God brought back to my remembrance the vision He gave me in London, standing on a glass bridge in the Grand Canyon. I shared it with Bryan, and he said, "Well, Google it."

Would you believe there is a glass bridge at the west side of the Grand Canyon! But it was another three hours on from where we were staying.

I said to Bryan, "We have to go there. It was in my vision."

We decided that we would see dawn break on Aimee's birthday. At 5 a.m. the next morning, the four of us were at the edge of the Grand Canyon, watching the sunrise break on the rocks. "Happy birthday, Aimee" was an experience for us all. We ate breakfast and then decided we would drive another three hours to find that glass bridge.

There was, of course, a cost to go onto the glass bridge. Bryan said if we did that, it would take all of our spending money.

I said, "Well, we need to. I need to relive the vision He gave me in London. Anyway, the kids had breakfast; they will be fine!"

We edged our way out onto the bridge. *Oh, my days! It's thousands of feet above the canyon floor!* Some people were having to crawl, not walk, out on it. The four of us held hands and said together, "We have made it. Thank You, Jesus, that You do speak to us with pictures, visions, and dreams."

God knew we would be doing this. He planned it, I'm sure, way back in London. So, nineteen months later, I lived out the vision He gave me in London when our first visa application was refused. This was an amazing, once-in-a-lifetime experience. Thank You, Jesus! And thank you, Andrew and Jen, for also being obedient.

After all the excitement, we were a little hungry and thirsty. We stood by the entrance to the one and only eating place—a BBQ restaurant.

Jonathan said, "Can we go in and eat?"

"Not at $40 a head, we can't," Bryan said.

Just then a waitress came up and said, "Can I have your meal tickets please?"

"We don't have any. Sorry," Bryan responded.

She looked at us and said, "Oh, are you English?"

"Yes."

"Come with me" and she led us through the restaurant to a table towards the back, overlooking the whole canyon.

"Here are some tickets. Enjoy your meal," she said with a smile (another angel).

The four of us just stared at each other thinking, *Did that just happen?* Then we ran to get our food.

After spring break, decisions were made about third-year internships. They were posted on the notice board. Bryan and I were the new interns for Healing School! Wow, God needed to come through. Only six weeks were left of second year.

Bryan had a wonderful mission trip to Columbia in April. He had a great time being stretched, as one is on mission trips. He came back with amazing testimonies of how God had showed up and given freedom to people and children on their trip.

We found out that we could do an extension on our visa, which meant not going back to England for the summer. It would be cheaper not to spend money on flights. But we had to show that magic $30,000 in the bank before immigration would extend our visa. We just had to believe that the Barn would sell. We had received news that there had been a number of people looking at it.

We had a long heart-to-heart with Vicki. She said, "I truly believe your house is going to sell. When it does, you can pay me back. But I'm expecting a miracle for you two!"

As Bryan and I discussed our options, we knew we were covered until the end of May by Vicki. We were determined that the first couple who had sponsored us would get every cent back once the Barn sold. We met with the international admissions coordinator as she was sorting out all of our international visa stuff. She needed us to show $30,000 in eight days!

"I really don't want to owe anyone else money. We already owe our parents some money from first year, the sponsors, and now Vicki. God, can't we do this ourselves somehow?"

As we went to bed that night, I asked Bryan, "Do we have anything anywhere we can pull on?"

Bryan said, "I went through everything last summer, Sue, when we sold all the stuff to get here."

As I woke up the next morning, I heard the Holy Spirit say, *"What about your ISA?"*

That was it, but it was so clear. I said to Bryan, "Do we still have ISA policies?"

In England, ISA is an investment plan. We took ours out when we changed our mortgage over about seven years ago. Bryan said, "I thought I went through everything, but I will call dad and check." (Bryan's dad held a lot of our paperwork.)

His dad called back a couple of hours later to say he had found some policies, but we would have to contact the company tomorrow. They were closed for the day. Bryan would need to call in the morning.

"I wonder how much we have in them," I said.

"I don't know," Bryan said, "but why didn't we remember these last year?"

The words came out of my mouth, "Because God had something else set up last year!"

We just looked at each other.

"Well," he said, "we will know in the morning when I call."

Miracle

Bryan came off the phone. He looked a bit stunned:

"Wow, we have just over 20,000 pounds, the equivalent of just over $30,000! We can do the extension on the visas, but I think we need to speak with Vicki first."

We chatted with Vicki, and she said, "I told you God would give you a miracle. You two need to do the visa extensions. The house will sell, and everyone will get their money back."

The next day, we told the international admissions coordinator that we could get the $30,000 for the visa. We had just three days until the deadline, but we were able to print off a bank statement to prove the money was in the bank.

She was amazed, "Wow, God really wants you two here, doesn't He?"she said.

We told Chris and Lisa. They were pleased too. Lisa was already planning our third year!

We had to then tell family that we wouldn't be back that summer. We were going to try to finish the third year. As you can imagine, they were sad but also happy we had found this money.

Daniel Amstutz, the director of Healing School, was happy; he wanted to plan two more Healing Schools on the Road and wanted our input. In addition, Healing School still happened every Thursday throughout the summer. It looked like we were going to be busy.

As second-year students, now it was all about graduation. As we were adding up our mission points, I realized I was short by $330, and Bryan was short $540. We needed to have those paid off or we wouldn't be able to walk the stage. It was momentarily discouraging because we had been serving at every opportunity. Three days before we had to either find the money or more points, we looked at the missions-point board and someone had paid them off! Another miracle!

May 18, 2013

Graduation Day
We were named the Class of Boldness!
(Bold as a Lion!)
Class Scripture: 1 John 4:17

To be honest, I couldn't believe we made it to this day.

Bryan's speech was great. Everyone had talked about Charis being "a bubble." Instead, Bryan referred to Charis as a greenhouse and shared a vision God had given him. He explained how we start as little seeds. As we grow, God can pot us on until we are ready to be planted in the garden of His choice.

Dear reader, this was the end of our second year at Charis, but it's not the end of our journey. The Barn hadn't sold, and we hadn't completed our third-year debt free yet. There was more to the journey and more promises to be fulfilled. This was where God showed us how to "just stand", trust, and believe in His Word and His promises. There was still more for us to learn on the next part of the journey.

Here is a great Scripture to stand on:

Ephesians 6:10-20 (NKJV): JUST STAND

Finally, my brethren, be strong in the Lord and in the power of His might. Put on the whole armor of God, that you may be able to stand against the wiles of the devil. For we do not wrestle against flesh and blood, but against principalities, against powers, against the rulers of the darkness of this age, against spiritual hosts of wickedness in the heavenly places. Therefore take up the whole armor of God, that you may be able to withstand in the evil day, and having done all, to stand.

Stand therefore, having girded your waist with truth, having put on the breastplate of righteousness, and having shod your feet with the preparation of the gospel of peace; above all, taking the shield of faith with which you will be able to quench all the fiery darts of the wicked one. And take the helmet of salvation, and the sword of the Spirit, which is the word of God; praying always with all prayer and supplication in the Spirit, being watchful to this end with all perseverance and supplication for all the saints—and for me, that utterance may be given to me, that I may open my mouth boldly to make known the mystery of the gospel, for which I am an ambassador in chains; that in it I may speak boldly, as I ought to speak.

JUST STAND

PART 3

Learning to Use My Wings

Chapter 17

SECOND YEAR GRADUATION REVISITED

Dear reader, I want to take a quick look back to Bryan's graduation speech. Do you remember I said that his speech had been great? What I haven't yet fully shared was the powerful vision God had given to him.

People who have experienced Charis often describe it as a "bubble." Students enter college, temporarily leaving the realities of their past lives behind. As students, the primary text we read is the Bible and we sit under teachers who share their life-altering experiences with the Gospel. For two years, students are hosed down, drenched, and saturated with the message of God's goodness, love, and grace. So to some extent, yes, Bryan and I had a sense that we were in an experience-bubble. However, God showed Bryan something different to share at graduation about the purpose of that experience.

Bryan's Greenhouse Vision

I [Bryan] *was standing outside this huge greenhouse about the size of a commercial aircraft hanger. As I walked in the doors, I saw a gentleman about halfway down. He looked and smiled at me and carried on repotting what looked like seeds into pots. As I looked down on the shelves, there were a variety of sizes of plant pots. The first ones just had soil in them. Then I could see little shoots in others, then bigger seedlings—and on and on as the plants were getting bigger and bigger. The gentleman walked down to the far end of the greenhouse, and there he picked up a large pot with a small tree in it and carried it outside.*

As I followed him out the door, suddenly, I was standing in a beautiful garden. It was a well-planned garden with different sections of different plants and trees. The gentleman smiled as he planted the small tree.

Then God shared with me, "You are not in a bubble; you are in a greenhouse. Everyone here is a handpicked seed; you are being planted, potted on, and nurtured until I can plant you where I want you to grow. Then, you will produce fruit that I have destined for you."

Then God went on to tell Bryan, *"You have a name for your ministry: 'Roots and Wings.' For once I have got your roots down deep in Me, I can give you the wings to fly."*

That was where the vision ended, but God had given us a name for our ministry—how exciting!

As you may remember, our class of 2013 was named the class of "boldness"; we were certainly that! This class produced a group of people that turned out to be stalwarts within Andrew's ministry. Some are in high -profile jobs to this day within AWM. Some have done amazing things around the world in many countries like Hong Kong, Australia, Scotland, and Africa, as well as many locations around the USA. We felt honored to be part of this class.

After graduation, we had to say goodbye to the friends who were doing only two years at Charis. Even after just two years in that environment, a lasting bond of friendship was created with classmates.

Although Vicki was going back to Canada for the summer to catch up on her house and family, praise God she was coming back for third year with us. As Bryan and I still couldn't work going into third year, we had our internships in Healing School to keep us busy during the summer. Chris and Lisa, who had watched our house and dogs for us when we were in England, were interns on the conferences team. Bryan and I were also due to travel with that team because we had been asked to oversee the prayer ministry. Since Daniel and Carlie were wanting to do two more Healing Schools on the Road, it seemed that we would be seeing more of America than we had anticipated. One of our trips would be to Minneapolis, Minnesota, and the other to San Jose, California.

We had lots to keep us busy, plus my parents were coming out for two weeks in July. I was so excited they had decided to come out to spend time with us. You see, we were in the midst of applying for our visa extensions, which meant we couldn't leave the States. It was ironic, really, that we had we tried so hard to get into this country and now we couldn't leave!

As interns, every Thursday we served at Healing School, which came with the added responsibility of overseeing the prayer ministry at the Summer Family Bible Conference, which that year would be at the Pikes Peak Center, downtown Colorado Springs.

The policy money had given us some breathing space, and I felt a slight relief from the pressure. With the summer months now here, surely the Barn was going to sell. "Thank You, Lord, that this will all be sorted out before we start our third year in Ministry School."

God was also showing us other things in addition to the vision He had given Bryan. He showed me that Bryan and I would be ministering together. He gave me pictures of us on stages in front of people. *Oh my days, that was scary!* I was just getting my head around giving the announcements each week at Healing School.

As I was connecting with the Holy Spirit, I was seeing more and more that there was a lot happening with Bryan and me spiritually. He told us that our ministry was His ministry. He said He would tell us when to launch it. We felt a little disappointed because He said that the time was not right yet. He said there was still ground to plow! *Hmmm, what does that mean, Lord?*

We knew one of the things we were to accomplish in third year was to develop a ministry plan for our ministry. So, in the natural, the timing to us seemed right. As we know, God's timing is not our own timing. So again, we just had to trust and wait patiently.

Healing School on the Road – Trip Two in America

As a lot of the students had left for the summer, we were light on the ground for help. Chris and Lisa had left to visit family. We had arranged with our friends to housesit while we were gone.

There were more forest fires again that summer. This time they were concentrated in Black Forest, north of Colorado Springs. We chatted with Daniel about our concerns about leaving our children at home alone. He agreed, as we were all traveling to Minneapolis on a shuttle bus, that they could come and help. We were amazed that there was enough room for us all to be in one hotel room. One of the benefits of American hotels is that they have two queen-size beds in each room. You don't get that in England! All we needed to do was cover all food expenses for the children. The crew was all set to leave: twelve of us on the shuttle bus headed out to Minneapolis. We had nineteen hours ahead of us on the road! Daniel and Carlie flew on ahead. Well, we were certainly seeing America—the interstate highways anyway!

The Charis Bible College in Minneapolis was excited to have students and staff visiting from the main campus in Colorado. *Would we beat our numbers of ministering to over 500 at the Kansas conference?* After the long drive, we were all flat-out setting up and getting ready for the event. All hands were on deck, including Aimee and Jonathan.

Once we were set up and ready to go, so many guests showed up to hear Daniel Amstutz and Carlie Terradez that we had to take a wall down in the conference center to make more room. At least the roof didn't have to be opened like in Capernaum when people couldn't get to Jesus (Mark 2:4). I'm sure the ministry did not have the proper insurance for that!

We also participated in a partner meeting. Andrew has always been the kind of minister who will wander into a crowd to meet those who come to see him. Bryan and I helped and enjoyed speaking with the partners. (Dear reader, it's funny now to think how all those steps led Bryan to the position he holds now, as director of ministry relations for AWM).

Again, we experienced such a great meeting in Minneapolis. We saw healings and heard testimonies of people receiving from God. I loved those road trips; people were so hungry to hear this message of truth that "GOD WANTS YOU WELL." I felt privileged to be part of all this. God was working in our hearts and changing us from the inside out also!

One thing that I was finding while ministering on the prayer line was how God was leading people to me who needed inner healing. It seemed like person after person came up to us with hurts that had been caused by a broken relationship. I felt unequipped in this area. I prayed, "God, show me how to minister to these people. What spiritual tools do I need?" From this trip to Minneapolis, we came away with lots of healing testimonies. Another Healing School on the Road was quickly planned for August in San Jose, California.

July was an exciting month, as my parents were coming out to visit Colorado. It would be their first time in the US. I could hardly wait until I would drive up to the Denver airport to pick them up. So much had happened to us in the year since we had seen them last. Since the weather was warm, we had a couple of short day trips planned for them. Needless to say, there were lots of hugs and tears when we picked them up. I have always had an amazing relationship with my parents. I feel very blessed and privileged.

That's why it has always been so hard for me to live away from England.

The activities of both the college and ministry quieted down in the summer. Our only obligation was to do Healing School on the Thursdays, so we were making the most of the two weeks we had with family. Garden of the Gods was our first trip out, a beautiful walk around the park. We came across a group of young adults who were just sitting on some rocks playing worship music, which seemed to echo around the park. *Wow, God, you are really trying to impress my parents!* We managed to cram all the local attractions into that day, including a day trip to Eleven Mile reservoir. We also took them to Walmart, where they decided everything looked gigantic, including the bags of crisps (chips)!

(Dear reader, we now have an American son-in-law. In summer 2019, we took him with us for his first trip to England, which he loved. But, in contrast with the supersizing of everything American, his comment on England was everything is so compact, like "Hobbit-land.")

Unfortunately, the time went far too quickly, but my parents got to meet a lot of people—Pastors Dan and Penny, and Chris and Lisa. When they went to Healing School, they met Daniel and Greg Mohr, as well as Barry Bennett. While Barry was speaking, my mum was in such awe!

I have decided that departures aren't nice, so enough said about that.

My mum left us by saying, "Well, at least it's only nine months; then you all will be home. It's only three years that you're here, right?"

With my parents gone, I had to turn my focus towards our next Healing School on the Road trip. We weren't sure how this was going to work. Most of the students had left for the summer. Daniel said the team was very small, and he was concerned that we wouldn't have enough people to run the event. He met with Bryan and me and said, "Hey, Aimee and Jonathan did a great job last time. Do you want to bring them again to help?"

"Yes, great," we said. "That will work."

Lisa agreed to look after the dogs, so we headed off towards the West Coast this time.

When you are driving for seventeen hours, you have time to think and chat. Bryan said to me he had looked at some stuff Elizabeth had sent him from Bethel. It was a ministry called "Sozo," and it was based on Luke 4:18, healing the brokenhearted. I liked the sound of that. I sort of felt it would be good for me too. So, we agreed to look into it when we got back.

As we were driving through California, we had arranged to meet Bryan's sister, Elizabeth, and her husband, Daniel, in Sacramento. They had driven down from Redding to meet us where we were stopping for a night. We also met up with our dear friend Andy and his wife, Jeri. Andy had gone through second year with us at Charis. He had taken Bryan under his wing and was like a spiritual father to Bryan. I'm still amazed how God does that; He makes a way for all these divine connections.

San Jose was an interesting trip. There were not as many people, and inadvertently, Carlie and Daniel had picked a weekend when there was a big festival going on. The atmosphere was different here. I was beginning to realize I was able to sense a lot more of what was going on spiritually around me. Of course, I would always check with the Holy Spirit by asking Him, "What are You showing me?"

People somehow just weren't as open to receive. In addition, Andrew wasn't as well known on the West Coast as in the other places we had visited. But some people did receive, so it was worth all our effort. Plus on the way back, we drove through San Francisco and got to have our photo taken at the Golden Gate Bridge. What a bonus!

Chapter 18

INTRODUCTION TO SOZO MINISTRY

Remember my prayer for wisdom on how to minister to those who needed inner healing? God gently started to teach me how to heal people's hearts, starting with my own. We all know that we should not let emotions rule us. But sometimes the things that have happened to us (lies and wounds) can cause us to not hear from God. They can also lead to physical problems in our bodies. I kept coming across this on the prayer lines, and I was earnestly asking the Lord, "What are we missing?"

Bryan and I have always listened to Bill Johnson from Bethel Church in Redding, California. He was sharing one day on heart issues and started to talk about *sozo*, a Greek word that can mean being made whole.

The Spirit of the Lord is upon me, because he hath anointed me to preach the gospel to the poor; he hath sent me to heal the brokenhearted, to preach deliverance to the captives, and recovering of sight to the blind, to set at liberty them that are bruised. (Luke 4:18, KJV)

This is a powerful scripture that demonstrates that Jesus not only came to heal us physically but emotionally as well. God spoke to me by saying that the devil is the one who oppresses us. God was showing me through this teaching on *sozo* that we have to take our authority even if it means facing some hurtful situations that we have buried. The word *sozo* appears over 100 times in the New Testament. God wants us to be free from our pasts, even if we are the ones who have caused the hurts and embraced the lies!

Bryan was excited because he had received a training course on Sozo ministry by mail from Bethel. He had also spoken with Teresa Liebscher. Teresa was one of the founders of Bethel's Sozo ministry and part of the leadership. (She was also the mother of Banning Liebscher of Jesus Culture, who happened to be a close friend of our brother-in-law Daniel). So, they connected and had a good chat. During their conversation, she told Bryan that after we had watched the course, she would put us in touch with the Colorado area coordinator for the Bethel Sozo network. This was a new area for us to explore, but it felt like God was leading us, so we followed.

As we studied, we could see that it was biblical and Holy Spirit lead. Sozo is not a counseling session but a time of interacting with Father, Son, and Holy Spirit for wholeness and freedom. Its main purpose is to connect people back to the Father. We began to realize that many people blame God for the things that go wrong. I know I had in the past. It seemed that the prayer I had prayed earlier about spiritual tools was being answered just in time. As we ministered, we were coming across more and more people who knew the Word but weren't able to get past their own hurts and wounds. It was preventing them from connecting with the Godhead.

The International Bethel Sozo Organization (IBSO) is located at Bethel Church in Redding. Sozo ministry began at Bethel Church in 1997. Later ISBO was formed for coordination and oversight as more and more churches wanted to add this ministry. Now it's quite a global network, having groups in over twenty countries worldwide.

What Bryan and I liked most about Sozo was that it had a scriptural foundation. So many inner healing ministries are led by feelings. The main goal with Sozo is to connect the believer back to the Godhead (Father, Son, and Holy Spirit) and bring wholeness to those you minister to. So many Christians believe lies that either the devil or other people have told them. This ministry is to expose the lies that Christians are believing that are crippling and disconnecting them and then reveal to them the truth about their relationship to God.

So, we finished the course and decided we would connect with the regional Bethel coordinator up in Loveland, Colorado, and find out our next steps.

September and the start of the school year were just around the corner. New students were arriving, and we were beginning to connect with the new internationals coming in. Lisa sent round a family from England, as we were still storing up furniture and kitchen equipment for incoming students. That's how the Entwistle family—Linda, Mick, and their son, Sam—entered our lives. They came from Bolton, in northern England. We straightaway hit it off, again laughing about the size of everything over here! I promised Linda a trip to Walmart; Mick and Sam were so excited to be here. They were like so many who come to Charis Bible College; they had given up everything to follow the call. Mick had been only two years away from his retirement as a fireman and had walked away from it. They had sold their home in England, so again, like us, it was all or nothing!

We had a great time chatting and getting to know one another over a cup of tea. We were grateful for good English tea bags. (Sorry to my American readers, but some of the American ones are just horrible!) We shared some of our testimony to date, which evoked from them the same response that we usually got— eyes and mouths wide open! They encouraged us in prayer about the sale of our home, and we were bonded from that time to now.

Chapter 19

WOW, RED LANYARD PEOPLE!

As Greg Mohr, the director of the Ministry School, was telling us the requirements of third-year and the responsibilities of wearing a red lanyard, I was thinking, *I can't do this!* But as ever, there was a little voice within saying, "Oh, yes, you can!"

It was true; I did feel different with that red lanyard on. I felt a responsibility to be a godly example to the blue lanyard (first-year) and green lanyard (second-year) students, whom we were already getting to know. Bryan and I had put our names down to teach a "late-bird" class to students. (This was a class taught in the afternoon after school was out.) Wow, we were big stuff now.

Over the summer, we had put together eight lessons on the topic of hearing from God. That had been such a part of our journey that we wanted to encourage others the same way. We had a growing awareness that activation had to play a strong part in our course. The activities I had done at the training course in England at Bath City Church in 2011 had changed me. There I learned that when we hear God for ourselves, and just not glean our revelation from a teacher, it is profound. That's what we wanted to get across to the students. We were really amazed; we had over thirty students sign up! Okay, so now we had to work out how to teach this.

I let Bryan lead off and then I would do the activities. Those eight weeks proved to be fun, and students really began to open up. We really enjoyed teaching. I was used to teaching my preschool children. In a way, I found this was similar; they were just bigger! Bryan and I were realizing that our style of teaching also required us to minister and pray together, which was new too.

We began the Fall 2013 term at the Elkton campus. We were all aware that this was going to be an interesting year. Andrew had been believing to get the college moved into the new Woodland Park campus by the start of the school year, but that wasn't able to happen. So, the plan now was to move us all up over the Christmas break. I felt sorry for those November students; they would have three weeks in the Elkton building off of Garden of the Gods Road in Colorado Springs, and then they would need to move up to Woodland Park. There were lots of questions from students on where to live: should they move to Woodland Park or remain in the Springs? Many had jobs down in the Springs and had signed leases on their homes. Chris and Lisa had decided over the summer to move up in anticipation of the move, so they were now driving down the hill to school. To our dismay, they weren't just around the corner anymore.

But Vicki and Mick, Linda, and Sam all still lived within five minutes of us.

We had decided to stay in the Springs because Aimee and Jonathan were attending CSCS. This was simplified because Aimee was driving now, and she could drive Jonathan to school. We also found it to be a bonus that it was always a good ten degrees warmer in the Springs than higher up the mountain!

October 2013: House Contract Number Three

We were getting ready again to sign paperwork on our house in the UK. I was certain this time it would go through. We were gutted when we had to lower the price. But we worked it all out; we could still pay back everyone we owed money to, with enough left over to finish out third year. The couple who had sponsored us in our second year weren't going to do a third year, so they had moved back to their home in another state. We reassured them that they would be repaid for all the money they had given us. Bryan and I kept our word on that. Even in the beginning, when they were sure God told them to sponsor us, I was firm on the fact that we needed to pay them back. God had clearly promised us we would be debt-free—that's what we were standing on!

We received a call from our neighbors in England; apparently, the night before, there had been the storm of all storms. The farm where our property was had been flooded, and the high winds had taken tiles off of our roof! This was the worst storm the South West of England had seen in fifteen years! *ARE YOU KIDDING ME! The media in the UK actually called it the 100-year storm.*

We then had phone calls from our lawyers to say that the people had tried to get to our house, but because the lane was flooded, they had decided to pull out of the deal—only twelve hours before they signed the contact! Bryan and I just looked at each other; we couldn't believe it. Everything had been going so well. We knew we had a month left on the policy money, but now what?

I said, "Well, Bryan, maybe we aren't meant to sell our home. Maybe we are meant to go back to England."

Bryan replied, "God told us we are going to be debt-free. How will that work if we go back to a mortgage?"

"Well," I said, "it's not looking too good here again."

We let Chris, Lisa, and Vicki know. Mick and Linda came round to pray with us. Vicki said she could help once the policy money ran out. I was just so tired of living like that. It was almost three years that we had been on this journey from the time when Bryan had given up his business. "God, I'm tired of this battle; I don't like owing money to people and family... What are we learning through this?"

Perseverance! Oh, Great...

Mick had a powerful prayer at this point:

"God, we know You are going to bring new buyers for Bryan and Sue, and within the next two weeks, they will have a new sale that won't fall through. IN JESUS' NAME!"

We all agreed on this. Now we had to sort out our missing tiles and whatever else the storm had done to our property. Our dear neighbors also told us to please come back, as they missed us.

At this time, we had a meeting with the Colorado-area Sozo coordinator, Pastor Bill Kline. He had invited Bryan and me to attend a Basic Sozo training weekend in Loveland, Colorado. We felt very strongly it would be good for us to go. With Aimee now driving, Bryan and I felt it would be okay for us to leave them for twenty-four hours. Mick and Linda said they could keep an eye out when they came round to walk the dogs. Mick and Linda loved to walk, and they loved our dogs. As Ute Valley Park was just around the corner from us, they would take them hiking with them. Evie and Poppi loved Mick and Linda; they had new walking buddies.

Bryan and I had changed so much over these past three years. We were growing closer, for sure, but there was still a part of both of our lives that we weren't letting God into. I sort of felt that even though we were searching for ways to help others, God was also stirring things in our own hearts.

We went through the training that weekend, and the last part of the schedule was left open for each person to have a Sozo session. It was interesting; I needed the truth on provision, so I knew that issue would come up. It was a very gentle style of ministry, with two ladies, one mainly leading it. In the session, Lady 1 would ask the Holy Spirit certain questions. Then I would listen and share with them what the Holy Spirit was telling me. I confirmed I didn't trust Him on provision. It also came up that I had a trust issue with Bryan. Okay, I knew that was true, but I couldn't hear why.

I was surprised after the session how tired I felt, but I knew things had broken off of me. I felt I had an understanding on provision now. It was very interesting. Lady 2 wrote down what are known as "love notes," things she heard the Spirit was saying to me through my responses to the questions. She handed them to me. They were all the positive things that God, Jesus, or the Holy Spirit had shown or told me during the prayer time. I got to keep those. I was amazed at how different I felt after the session. I felt lighter, as if a load had been taken off of me.

When I asked Bryan how his session went, he said the same. The Holy Spirit had worked on identity and provision with him also. I found all of this very interesting. Bill Kline told us that he felt we had a calling to minister this way. He instructed us to go home, pray about it, chat with our pastors in the Springs, and get back to him.

I knew also that the Holy Spirit was bringing back to me a time in our marriage when life wasn't good. I was quiet as we drove home and over the next couple of days. Actually, I didn't think much about the house either. God was stirring things in my heart, and I felt strong enough now to deal with whatever it was He was showing me.

Third year was busy, and our studies were on a different level than they had been the first two years. In addition, our Healing School internship was taking up a lot of time.

Chapter 20

A Transition of Heart

Three weeks after we had received news that the sale had fallen through, we had new buyers. They offered us 10,000 pounds less than the asking price. At that point, I didn't care. We said okay, but we responded that we wouldn't give them anything that was on the property.

Elizabeth and Daniel were planning on moving back to England, so we arranged for the contents of the estate to be removed and stored. Elizabeth and Daniel would be able to have that once they were back in England.

Thanksgiving Day

We introduced Mick, Linda, and Sam to the American holiday of Thanksgiving. Chris and Lisa brought some American dishes. They were the only Americans there, surrounded by a bunch of English students from Charis—and one Canadian.

We also had a big Thanksgiving dinner meal at HMI Church for all the people who didn't have a place to go on Thanksgiving. As part of our practicum for third year, we were assistant pastors at the church for Dan and Penny Funkhouser. Dan and Penny had been amazing and such a support to us. It was discussed that we would be taking over the operational side of the church for them.

I was not getting my hopes up, but it so far so good with these buyers. They seemed to be steaming through the paperwork. We were informed that contracts could be ready by mid-December. Dare I say we could be all done by Christmas?

To be honest, we were so busy with church and college that the house sale had moved to a back shelf in my mind. Or was it that Sozo session, where I had made a transition in my heart? It had been only after that when I felt I could trust God to take care of it.

I kept looking at all the new November students, walking around with deer-in-headlights looks on their faces. Another couple from England arrived, Adam and Cathrin. She was from Germany. They hadn't been married that long. Mick and Linda had taken them into their group of friends. Other internationals like Bruce and Sarah were from South Africa. They lived in the same apartment block as Mick and Linda.

We were really encouraging the new students to connect. They didn't know it yet, but they would need one another as support on their journey. That's what the body of Christ is about, isn't it?

Bryan's parents FaceTimed us to say they wanted to give us a chance to use their timeshare in Florida for a week over Christmas break. Wow, we could have done with a vacation. It'd been a few years since we had one!

We thought we could actually do a road trip to Florida. (Stupid Brits, thinking that would be fun!) It would be a lot cheaper than flying. Mick and Linda agreed to move in over Christmas and housesit the dogs. Chris and Lisa would also come and have Christmas dinner with them. So, we were set; we would leave December 17.

We had an extra week off of school as the staff were moving up to Woodland Park. So, college wasn't starting until January 10. Then there would be a season up the mountain in Woodland Park in 2014 for us all.

THE HOUSE SOLD—in Just
Two Years and Nine Months!

December 18, 2013

We had a call from our lawyers as we were driving through Kansas: All contracts had now been signed. The buyers moved in the next day, as they wanted to be in for Christmas. So, we called our parents, family, and friends, to share the great news that the house finally SOLD! In a way, our families had mixed feelings. I understood that, but on this side of the Atlantic, there was a lot of celebrating and thank-yous to hand out to all our family and friends who had stood with us in prayer and in emotional and financial support. *Great rewards back to you all!*

We told Aimee and Jonathan that we'd celebrate, so we stopped at IHOP for pancakes! I felt a wave of relief come over me, realizing we could finally pay back the money we owed people. It would take a few days to sort out finances, pay one big lawyer bill and pay off a mortgage, as well as give back the money to the couple who had sponsored us in second year. Finally, we would pay back some family members and then we'd see what was left! But within a few days, we would be debt-free.

We arrived in Orlando for our weeklong vacation. I just felt like I wanted to sleep for a week. We all felt like a great weight had been removed. We had a fun day with Aimee and Jonathan, going to the Everglades to see the alligators. It was a cool ride on an airboat. The children decided they were too old for Disney, so we headed to Busch Gardens. We had a fun day there as well. At Busch Gardens, we met friends that we had been students at Charis with, Myron and Kathy. They only did the two years before moving back to Florida to be near family again.

The drive back to Colorado was very, very long. Aimee and Jonathan decided that they wouldn't want to do that long of a road trip again!

January 2014 – Wow, Another Year in America

Once we got back from Florida, we still had a week before school started in its new location up the mountain. We needed to sort out the last of the house finances—Not a lot left, Lord. It was amazing how little was left once we paid everyone back every pound and dollar! *Sorry, Lord, but we can't help looking at what we don't have … rebuke coming!*

"Bryan and Sue, stop looking at what you don't have, but bless what you have!"

The Lord lead us to Matthew 14:13-21, how Jesus blessed the loaves and fishes.

And Bryan and Sue said in unison: "YES, LORD."

Dear reader, I know you are going to think this next statement is a weird thing to say, but I felt like the house sale was anticlimactic. By the time the sale was finally over, God had provided for us beyond our imagination and we knew we could always trust Him on provision. People at the church were so happy for us that it was finally over. Dan wanted Bryan and me to share at church the next Sunday. So, we would be ministering together on "God, You are our source."

> And my God shall supply all your needs according to His riches in glory by Christ Jesus.
>
> Philippians 4:19 NKJV

The next day, I spent a long time in prayer.

After that time, God said to me, "So, Sue are you ready to open up your heart to Me?"

Chapter 21

EVERY LOVE STORY IS BEAUTIFUL, BUT OURS IS MY FAVORITE

God was gently reminding me of the time when my heart had been closed to Bryan. We weren't in a good place with our marriage; this was during our thirties. Remember I had only asked Jesus into my life at fourty! I wanted my life to change, and boy, did that happen! But I knew that there were hurts and lies in my heart that God wanted to uproot.

After a few days of seeking Him in quiet prayer, God said, "How can you heal others when you still have a broken heart, Sue?"

As I pondered His question and prayed, God showed me a scripture.

> *Do not remember the former things, Nor consider the things of old. Behold, I will do a new thing.* (Isa 43:18-19, NKJV)

The things we go through can either help us grow or hold us back. If we're focused on the things that have happened to us in the past or the mistakes that we've made, then we're not focused on what God's doing now. Jesus said, *The thief comes only to steal and kill and destroy;* [Don't I know! That is our past life.] *I have come that they may have life, and have it to the full"* (John 10:10, NIV).

Not every bad thing in our past was caused by our Enemy, the "thief." Sometimes it is our own choices that open the door to the devil. But if we don't deal with those doors, he can keep us trapped and steal our future from us. We won't be able to live our lives to the fullest. But when we allow God to help us process, grow, and move on from our past experiences, we can step into the amazing plans that God has for us. God can lift us up, even when we've reached rock bottom. His strength is revealed and released in our weakness. As God said to Paul, *"My grace is sufficient for you, for my power is made perfect in weakness"* (2 Cor 12:9, NIV).

The Father specializes in using people who have faced rejection. He used Joseph, a man thrown into a pit by his brothers and written off by his father as dead. He used David, a shepherd boy alienated and overlooked by his family. David made some pretty big mistakes regarding his own life decisions. He committed adultery and murder but was still described as a man after God's own heart! Jesus was the stone the builders rejected (Psa 118:22), and He went on to become the chief cornerstone (Luke 20:17). God can do the same for us. He has a plan for each of our lives. As we spend time dealing with the past and becoming fully repented (or turned) to Him, He'll reveal the new things He has in store for us.

At my turning point, God said to me, "Sue, I have so much more for you and Bryan, but this one area has to be worked through in both of your hearts. Remember Jeremiah 29:11-12? The plans I have are good plans for you both. I have already sent you the tools you need (Sozo), but now you have to be open and honest with each other."

I think you've been with me long enough on this journey, to come to the same conclusion as me: God does know everything. We can't keep secrets from Him! God wants the best for us. He will always fulfill His promises to us, but He is not obligated to fulfill our full potential. We must cooperate with Him for that to come to pass!

My answer was, "Yes Lord, I want all you have for Bryan and me. I know that even though it will be painful to walk through, You will be with us."

I heard Jesus reply, "I do not look at your past. I paid for all that on the cross. You both have to forgive each other, move into a newness in your marriage, and fulfill the plans I have for you."

You see, God isn't only interested in the final destination. He is interested in our transformation along the way. I would say that most people have a past, especially if they accept Jesus as Lord and Savior later in life.

The revelation I had in that moment was grace is a person, not a substance or energy-force given to us by God so that we can make it through trials. Jesus' unconditional love for us is not a love the world understands. Even as Christians, we sometimes don't fully understand what grace means. When Jesus went to the cross, He said, "It is finished." That means finished. Final. No more. Don't look back. Forgive yourself and forgive others! This was the mind-blowing revelation that I couldn't wait to share with Bryan.

Bryan and I had to address the issues we had carried with us from those years. We had already started to experience the power of forgiveness. God had shown us this together, in Matthew 18, in the parable of the unforgiving servant. I was always troubled by verses 34-35:

> *And his master was angry, and delivered him to the torturers until he should pay all that was due to him. "So My heavenly Father also will do to you if each of you, from his heart, does not forgive his brother his trespasses."* (NKJV)

My question (probably like yours) was, why would Father God put us in prison?

Like a loving Father, He answered me, "Sue, I'm not the one putting you in prison; you are. You have the keys to unlock the door. It's called forgiveness. The devil wants to keep you in unforgiveness. I want to set you free."

In that moment, I finally understood that when we forgive people, we take back power from the devil. He can't keep us under offense, bitterness, resentment, or regrets. We do that to ourselves.

So later, in a beautiful time in prayer with Bryan, we forgave each other for our past words, choices, and actions. It was like the Holy Spirit was washing over us, and through us, and we were clean.

So many of us push stuff down in our hearts, praying we won't have to face our past mistakes. The Good News is that Jesus already paid for them, so why are we holding on to them? Jesus works in our present and our future. If we dwell on our past, we undervalue the cost of Jesus going to the cross for us.

My heart is, for anyone who is struggling with their past, I encourage you right now to hand it to God. He says in Matthew 11:28-30 (NIV):

> *Come to me, all you who are weary and burdened, and I will give you rest. Take my yoke upon you and learn from me, for I am gentle and humble in heart, and you will find rest for your souls. For my yoke is easy and my burden is light.*

Then Bryan and I prayed a powerful prayer together that we had first experienced through our Sozo training. I feel the anointing on this prayer is strong, and I would encourage any of you readers to stop here and take time to pray. You won't be the same as you turn this next page.

Please pray the following prayer:

> *Holy Spirit, please show me any area of my heart where I have unforgiveness toward another person. Lord, I repent and ask You to forgive me for bitterness, resentment, or offenses I have been holding against_____.*
> *I forgive each person I have named, and I ask You to bless them. Please forgive me for any agreements I have made with the lies of the Enemy. I break those agreements now. Thank*

You for forgiving me and cleansing me with Your blood, Lord Jesus. I receive Your healing touch and ask You to replace my wounded emotions with Your healthy emotions. AMEN.

While unforgiveness is a door that will open your life to the Enemy, soul ties are another area that can hold you back from what God fully has for you. A soul tie is a link between two people. Unhealthy soul ties can cause a broken heart. God wants to break those chains so you can walk in freedom.

*Father, if I have formed any ungodly **soul ties** with the following people in any manner, I ask You to forgive me. I choose to free my mind, will, and emotions from each of the following people. [Take the time to say their names out loud.] Please forgive me for holding unforgiveness toward them. I forgive them now and ask You to bless them with Your truth that will set them free. I release them to You now. I put the blood of Jesus between myself and each person I have named as well as every demon that has had any influence in this situation. I ask this in the precious name of the Lord Jesus Christ. AMEN.*

Freedom is now yours. Remember it's your choice.

Chapter 22

February 2014:
New Beginnings

We met with Pastors Dan and Penny and discussed with them what we had walked through. They were so full of grace. We also said we wanted to have a Sozo training course weekend at HMI Church. Bryan and I had a passion to set people free. Pastor Dan said he would like to meet with Pastor Bill Kline to discuss that idea further, so we made those arrangements.

Penny was very excited when I shared with her about Sozo, but she was most excited about how it had helped Bryan and me. A couple of weeks later, Pastor Bill Kline came and met with Dan and Penny. We all had a great meeting and arranged to run a Sozo conference at HMI Church. The event would be next month, and Bryan and I would do all the organizing.

At this time, Pastor Bill asked us, "So, what are your plans after Charis?"

So much had gone on over the last couple of months, we told him, we hadn't yet given it much thought. We explained that, with our home now sold in England, if we went back, we would have to try to get jobs and find somewhere to live. With not having worked for three years, all our savings and the remainder of the house money would be gone by the end of summer!

Pastor Bill said to us, "What's the desire of your hearts?"

"Wow, we hadn't thought about that, to be honest," Bryan and I answered.

We knew that ministry-wise, we wanted to see people set free, connected back to God, and fall in love with His Word. That was what we wanted ministry-wise.

"Okay," Bill said, "but what about you as a family? What do you want? You have not because you ask not. Remember, He gives us the desires of our hearts" (Psa 37:4).

Bryan and I looked at each other; that was a question we needed to ask our Father.

Taking our cue from that evening, over the next few days, we asked Aimee and Jonathan, "What do you two want? Your crazy parents took you on this journey, but as a family, we all need to decide what we want to do next. We all need to be in unity."

After a couple of days, the children said, "Actually, we want to stay in America a bit longer."

Strangely enough, I was feeling that way too. Then Aimee said, "I want to finish my junior year in May. I want to graduate high school here. It would be so hard for me to go back now to England and finish my schooling."

Jonathan also said he had made friends over the last three years. He was moving into freshman year. He could go back into the English system, for sure, but Aimee would be in between school and college. Aimee even suggested she could move in with her best friend, Beth, and finish CSCS if we three decided to go back. CSCS, had a lot of international students. If she stayed with Beth's family, she would change to an F-1 visa student, so that could easily be arranged if needed.

Bryan said, "Well, whatever we do, we do as a family. We have come this far together; I don't think God will split us up now."

Third year was going so well. I could hardly believe we only had ten weeks left at Charis. We were in the midst of our ministry group projects. Bryan was on the team with Ricky Burge, who was developing a Charis plan for Uganda. What a life story he has.

(Dear reader, you can check him out on Andrew's website on the *Inside Story*: https://www.awmi.net /video/series/the-inside-story/?id=S81WXfnU

I was working with a group whose vision was developing a children's church curriculum empowering youth in the supernatural. These projects were "stretching times" for all the third-year students, as Greg Mohr used to say!

We were also looking for second-year student candidates who would take over our Healing School internship. We found a great couple that we knew would be awesome, Tim and Connie March. We chatted with Daniel Amstutz, who said he thought that they would be good too. It seemed strange to hand this over. Healing School had been such a big part of our lives throughout our time at Charis.

Bryan and I had another meeting with Pastors Dan and Penny. They also wanted to know what our plans were for after third year. We told them what we had discussed with the children and that they wanted to stay a little longer here. Penny asked me how I felt about that. I explained to her that, strangely, I was also being led that way.

Dan said, "Well, we don't want you guys to leave, either; you are such a blessing to us and the church."

And then he followed by asking, "So, what do we need to do to keep you guys here a bit longer?"

Bryan explained that we need to go through another visa process. We would need to change from M-1 visas to R-1, religious workers visa. Dan asked Bryan to research that and come back to him.

Over the next couple weeks, we got in contact with an immigration lawyer to find out what the process was to change over our visas. We had to start the process thirty days before our M-1 visas were due to run out. Our visas, would expire on June 15, so we had time, but we had to make that decision soon. We realized that by changing over visas we would again be "in process." That would be like a second third-year if we extended the M-1 visa. It also meant we couldn't exit the country while we were "in process."

Ahhh, it would be another summer when we wouldn't be able to travel home. The process would take about six months. Immigration would have to visit Dan's church, and we would have to list all the jobs we do there. It would cost us around $7,000 as a family, so if we did that, it would leave us very short over the summer.

Dan said, "Let's do this. HMI Church will sponsor you as associate pastors." We would both be working twenty hours a week. *Wow, God, that scripture came back to us, about how we have not because we ask not* (James 4:2).

Chapter 23

NEW DIRECTION

By that time, April had arrived and we began to realize that we would have to share this news with our family in England. They were very good and understood about the children's schooling. They also said that they felt God did have more for us in America, but they hoped one day we would be back in England.

That's the thing; we can make plans, but God directs our paths (Prov 16:9).

We asked Dan and Penny if we could renew our wedding vows; this had been on both our hearts. We knew what we had walked through over the past few months. We both felt different—more together than ever. So, since we were due to celebrate our twenty-third wedding anniversary on April 20 and it was a Sunday, Dan said he thought it would be awesome for us to do this with the church. The next week, we stood up in front of the HMI church family and renewed our wedding vows to each other.

It felt so special. Dan blessed our wedding rings again, and we had Aimee and Jonathan as our witnesses. I could feel Jesus standing there with us. Dan talked about the cord of three strands that is not easily broken, from Ecclesiastes 4:12. I knew that Jesus was the center of our marriage now.

Don't ever think you have made too many mistakes or wrong choices. Jesus is always there when you are willing to repent. Love does cover all (1 Pet 4:8).

Things were moving quite quickly. On the visa stuff, we had to gather all our paperwork and send it into Immigration. Also, we were telling a few of our close friends that this was the door God had opened up. I was relieved that finally, we can have a paid job! After the last three years, our friends were happy for us, but it was with mixed feelings.

Vicki for sure was heading back to Canada. She needed to go back to attend to her house and properties she had there. Chris and Lisa were planning on starting a Charis Bible College in Scotland, but they knew it would take them a couple of years before they would be ready to leave. Mick, Linda, and Sam were going into second year. We had other friends from the church, like John and Cheryl. They were interested in helping us launch the Sozo ministry at HMI. One of things we had to do was to apply to be part of the Bethel Sozo network. That would be approved just before our Sozo conference.

The Sozo conference was great. Pastor Bill brought a team with him from Loveland. It was a two-day training conference, on a Friday afternoon and all day Saturday. We had sixty-four people come from the church, plus a few Charis students. We saw some amazing ministry and people being set free. This set us on fire. Again, freely you receive freely you give.

I just couldn't believe we were graduating third year in three weeks. We were underway with the visa process with HMI Church support now. It would still be tight on money, only working part-time, but we understood that was all the church could do for now. We also knew that God was more than capable of supplying our needs.

I felt, again, God say, "There is another door opening up for you."

We were chatting with Daniel about transitioning Healing School over to Tim and Connie, but this had become so much more than just an internship. The college was growing and developing in a lot of areas. The move up to Woodland Park had opened up a lot of positions. Some of our classmates were being offered positions, which was awesome.

They asked Bryan and me if we would still like to travel with the conference team. We could do it, as we were working only part-time for the church. Again, the conference team was expanding. Andrew was doing more away conferences. Carlie had transferred to the conference team after that school year. Lots of changes were ahead. Bryan had developed a system for the prayer ministry on the travel team, as well as assisting them on the operational side.

It was just before third-year graduation that Larry Bozeman, the then-conference director, approached Bryan and said, "So, I understand you are planning on staying in America a bit longer. How would you and Sue like to work for Andrew Wommack Ministries? We have seen how you both have served over the past couple of years. Go away and pray about it, but come back to me in a week, as I need to advertise a couple of part-time positions."

Wow, God, I'm guessing our time is not over in America. We both prayed about it, and then we went to see Dan and Penny. As our visas were in-process with them as sponsors, we wanted their advice. They said the church could only offer us part-time positions, so if AWM could offer us part-time as well, that would for sure give us what we would need to stay here as a family. But the R-1 we had was with HMI Church, so if AWM wanted us, then they would have to do the same process and apply for a part-time R-1.

We met up with Larry Bozeman to let him know we were interested, but we would also need the ministry to sponsor us in the R-1 process. They agreed, so we were in visa processing now with AWM as well.

It was amazing the doors God had opened up to us. All I kept thinking back to was that time in January when God said, "I can only do what I have planned for you if you trust Me and deal with your broken heart." God has so much for us, but sometimes He can only move after we let go of the baggage that is holding us back!

Graduation Day – May 17, 2014

Bryan and I received extra awards of honor for leadership in our third year. We walked across the stage together with a new adventure in our hearts. What was God going to do next?

One thing was for sure, THE BEST WAS YET TO COME!

Epilogue

THE END, BUT NOT REALLY ...

Dear reader, October 29, 2019, marked the tenth anniversary of me giving my life to Jesus. Of those ten years, eight years of them have been lived in America. So, what else has God done as we travel on this journey with Him?

After receiving our R-1 visas, we traveled back to visit family in England for Christmas that year. At that time, it had been four years since we had had an English Christmas. We had missed the blessing of all our English foods and traditional Christmas fun. It was a wonderful time, just being together, but at the same time we knew we had all changed. I think for our families, this was hard; they now knew we were putting God first, and for some, they didn't understand. I had always put family first; the love for them all hadn't changed, just our focus. Goodbyes were still hard, and it is true as they say, "You can take the girl out of the country, but not the country out of the girl."

Bryan and I are approaching thirty years of marriage, as we both now turn fifty! We are excited as to what God has ahead for us on this adventure together with Him. Remember, as Bryan and I say, God knows our destination, but what He's really interested in is our transformation along the way!

Regarding family—Well, Aimee graduated from high school and decided she wanted to go to Moody Bible Institute in Chicago. Again, I had to trust Jesus to take care of her, and He did. While in Chicago, she learned a lot about the Scriptures, but after one year, she said it was not for her. In October of 2016, she came to us, saying God was leading her to go to Charis. Like Bryan and I, she began as a November student. Aimee kept telling us, "I'm not going to be part of *Charis Bridal College*. I'm only doing a year while I sort out what to do next!"

Little did Aimee know at the time, but God had another plan—a nice young man from Wray, Colorado, also started as a November student that year. James and Aimee started to date during February of 2017. They got engaged during their second year, and three days after graduation, they were married (Charis Bridal College!). So, yes, we have an American son-in-law.

Jonathan also graduated high school, three years behind Aimee. Along the way, his school soccer team went on a mission trip to Ecuador, which he loved. He wanted a gap year after high school to decide what he wanted to do. He now works currently as a valet at a five-star resort in Colorado Springs.

I have learned that my children belong to Jesus. We have to trust Him to guide them. It's hard as parents, but really, we have to allow them to make their own choices. We have to be there to love them and guide them through those choices, just as God does for us.

As you may remember, God gave us the name for our ministry—Roots and Wings—while we were in Charis. He told us to wait on Him and He would show us when to launch it. We waited, and He showed us in the summer of 2016 that it was the time.

We were getting ready to renew our R-1 visas with both HMI Church and AWM. A visa can be held thirty months before renewal. Once we had renewed them for a second time, we applied for green cards. Then, both Bryan and I were offered full-time jobs with AWM and Charis. In 2015, I worked for Charis' Education Department with Greg Mohr. Later, I became his executive assistant when Greg moved up as director of the college.

However, all our new jobs were taking time away from our church duties.

We wanted to chat with Dan and Penny about this and about what God had shown us regarding our own ministry. Dan has such a heart to see people launched into their callings. He is a pioneering pastor that equips the saints to do the work of the ministry. They agreed that God was leading us to do our own ministry. God had also opened up the door for another couple to come in and support them on the operational side of the church. They said they were sad, but they were also happy for us. We weren't walking away from HMI and just handing over the duties. However, it was decided we would not renew the R-1 visa with the church. We would only renew the AWM visa, as we both worked full-time and only needed to apply for one. Although it was a big change for us, by stepping down from church we could also see what doors God wanted to open up for Roots and Wings.

By the end of October 2016, we had already received our 501(c)3 charitable tax status for Roots and Wings. *Wow, that only took six weeks to come through.* God's timing again.

Bryan worked on setting up a website, and we would get our board together to pray about how God wanted Roots and Wings to work. We didn't have any idea! We just knew it would involve traveling, ministering, and teaching.

Our first teaching invitation came from Wyoming in March of 2017. After that, God has been faithful to open up many doors for us, to churches as well as Charis extension schools. Bryan and I have ministered in Europe and England, and we are heading off to the Far East later 2020. We love to teach, travel, and encourage the church leadership, the body of Christ and the lost. We know what it's like to be on a journey with God because we still are! Never underestimate what God can do if you say yes to Him.

We have ministered in some great churches as well as made some great ministry friends. It's so important as the body of Christ to build each other up. We know that God has blessed us so greatly, and we know that Roots and Wings is His ministry. We are His vessels, and it's cool to see what He can do through us.

This is the second book we have written. The first one Bryan worked on was called *God's Airwaves.* It takes readers on a journey into hearing from God for themselves. We encourage you to take a look at it. It is a great tool for a Bible study.

HMI Church's Sozo ministry is still going strong and releasing people into freedom. It's now led by our dear friends John and Cheryl Bullock. Bryan and I still minister when we can, and we have a passion for setting the captives free.

At the time this of this writing, I have worked for Charis for five years as Greg Mohr's assistant. Bryan is currently the director of ministry relations for Andrew Wommack Ministries and Charis Bible College.

Some Last Thoughts

Perhaps as you have read this book, you've come to realize there is more to knowing Jesus than just going to church. Maybe you are realizing you don't have a living relationship with Jesus. That's what this journey is all about—discovering that it's not about religion; it's about having a relationship with the one true God who died for you so that you could have eternal life. Every single human being has the opportunity to accept Jesus and have eternal life in heaven. That is a given for all mankind. I know not everyone will accept this free gift. That's what breaks my heart.

At the start of our journey, God gave me this scripture: Matthew 22:14—"*Many are called, but few are chosen.*"

Once you are born again, we also have to consider the call to be a disciple. That's where you take up the cross and follow Him. Is there a difference? Yes. Bryan and I could have stayed in England, worked things through, carried on with our church duties, and had a comfortable life. God stirred something deeper in our hearts, and that's why we took this journey. If we hadn't done that, God wouldn't have loved us any less. God's heart is for all to know Him. It's not what you do for God; instead it's allowing God to work through you so you can show others His love for them.

So, my request to you as you are reading this, if you don't know Jesus, pray this prayer sincerely. Mean it with all your heart. In Romans 10:9-10, it says that whoever calls on the name of the Lord will be saved. We just simply have to believe and receive:

"Dear Father God, I know I'm a sinner, and I ask for Your forgiveness. I believe Jesus Christ is Your Son. I believe that He died for my sins and that You raised Him to life. I want to trust Him as my Savior and follow Him as my Lord, from this day forward. Guide my life. Now that I have received my salavtion, I pray to You, Father God, for Your power of the bapitism of the Holy Spirit to come and fill me. By faith I receive it right now. You are welcome into my life, Holy Spirit. I pray this in the name of Jesus. Amen."

Congratulations! You are now filled with God's supernatual power; your life will never be the same!

Last thing for you to ponder on...

"Keep your heart filled with faith and your actions filled with obedience."

Further Resources to Explore:

Websites:

Roots and Wings Ministries International
www.rootsandwingsmi.org

Andrew Wommack Ministries
www.awmi.net

Charis Bible College
www.charisbiblecollege.org

Authors and books that inspired us on our journey:

The Holy Bible, NKJV

Andrew Wommack

- *Spirit, Soul & Body*

- *The Believer's Authority*

- *God Wants You Well*

Greg Mohr

- *Prosperous Soul*

- *Your Healing Door*

Barry Bennett

- *Did God Do This to Me?*

- *Hearing from God*

Bill Johnson

- *Face to Face with God*

- *Hosting His Presence*

- *The Supernatural Power of a Transformed Mind*

Danny Silk

- *Keep Your Love On*

- *Culture of Honor*

- *Powerful and Free*

Graham Cooke

- *Prophetic Wisdom* series

Dawna De Silva and Teresa Liebscher

- *SOZO: Saved—Healed—Delivered*

Andrew Murray

- *Humility*

'ef Hetland

'*ealing the Orphan Spirit*

GOD'S AIRWAVES

A Practical Guide to Tuning In to God's Voice Through Modern-Day Prophecy

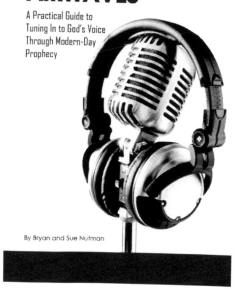

By Bryan and Sue Nutman

Powerful Book and Bible Study

In this powerful book, Bryan and Sue Nutman lay a biblical foundation and give practical opportunities for believers to hear God's voice. *God's Airwaves: A Practical Guide to Tuning In to God's Voice Through Modern-Day Prophecy* takes you on an incredible spiritual journey while training you to demonstrate the Father's power and grace with an accuracy that portrays His heart of love for others.

In this book, discover:

- how to hear God's voice and what He sounds like to you individually.
- how to pay attention to the Holy Spirit and respond to His leading.
- how to judge correctly what you see, hear, and sense.
- how the Holy Spirit wants to interact with you and others.
- how to develop a passion for prophecy that will change the lives of those around you.

You can get this book and other materials on our website at **rootsandwingsmi.org.**